2 95
6
T.2/

The Charles Fillmore Concordance

AN EXPANDED INDEX TO THE WRITINGS OF CHARLES FILLMORE

compiled by Clinton E. Bernard
editorial revision by Jeffrey Fischer

NITY BOOKS
UNITY VILLAGE, MISSOURI

THE CHARLES FILLMORE CONCORDANCE

an expanded index

to the writings of Charles Fillmore

The Charles Fillmore Concordance was compiled by Clinton E. Bernard, with editorial revision by Jeffrey Fischer.

Copyright 1975 by
Unity School of Christianity

Preface

Charles Fillmore's teachings are known to millions of people, who follow them for daily, practical guidance. The purpose of this Concordance is to help the student get closer to the spirit of Mr. Fillmore's work . . . and to provide a quick reference to the thousands of practical ideas that Charles Fillmore put into his books.

This book, together with the ten volumes of Charles Fillmore's writings (plus the compilation *Dynamics for Living*), will make a wonderful reference library for any Truth student. Here is inspiration, and explanation of many hidden, practical truths in the Bible. Charles Fillmore was able to interpret and make of practical and inspirational benefit, to all who wish to understand, the deep significance of the Biblical symbols.

Emmet Fox, author of many books that are widely read by the general public, and who also had for a number of years a large following in his church in New York City, was a great admirer of Charles Fillmore. When Dr. Fox visited Unity in Kansas City, in 1944, he wrote:

"I look upon Charles Fillmore as being among the prophets. He has given us something that the great prophets have given us. A prophet is, you know, one who has certain contact with God in a very rare degree and gives that out to his fellowmen. He is a broadcasting station for God. We all know the great prophets in the Bible, and there have been a few outside of them. He [Charles Fillmore] is one of the great men of this generation, although unknown as such to the world at large. The things which really are his are not the things which are so apparent on the surface. I am one of his spiritual children."

Note

The ten Charles Fillmore books are identified in this Index by means of initials, as follows:

ASP	Atom-Smashing Power of Mind
CH	Christian Healing
JC	Jesus Christ Heals
KL	Keep a True Lent
MG	Mysteries of Genesis
MJ	Mysteries of John
P	Prosperity
TM	The Twelve Powers of Man
TP	Teach Us to Pray
TT	Talks on Truth

Each entry refers to subject matter in one or more of the ten books. For instance, the following entry

Abundance, KL: 101, 183; affirming, P: 93, 121-122, 126, 169-170. (See *Prosperity*)

indicates that there are references to "abundance" on pages 101 and 183 of *Keep a True Lent;* and references to "affirming abundance" on pages 93, 121-122, 126, and 169-170 of *Prosperity.* "See *Prosperity*" indicates that under the index entry for "Prosperity" the student may find other references that he will find helpful in studying the subject of abundance.

A

Aaron, ASP: 83

Abanah, river Damascus, TP: 149

abdomen, CH: 75
   as seat of renunciation (elimination), TM: 16, 21,
      158-160

Abel, (mind), MG: 58, 60-62, 65, 70 (see Mind)

Abel-mizraim, (meadow) MG: 373, 374

Abida, MG: 203

abilities, (mental and spiritual), ASP: 13

Abimael, MG: 107

Abimelech (will), MG: 171-174, 180,
    181, 212-213, 216 (see Will)

Abraham, MG: 11, 113, 120, 122, 128, 130, 143, 144,
    155, 156, 160, 164, 167, 181, 189, 200, 211; MJ: 33,
    34, 89, 92; TT: 156; TM: 92 (see Abram; Faith; and
    Sarah)
  and tithing, MG: 134-138
  as demonstrator of Christ in man, MG: 115; MJ: 92
  as representing faith, MG: 116-119, 123, 124, 127, 134,
    135, 140-144, 148, 151-152, 157-159, 161, 162, 165,
    168, 169, 171-187, 192-195, 199, 201, 202, 204, 214,
    216
  as symbol of faith and obedience, MG: 201; TM: 25, 26
  bosom of, TT: 156
  burial place of, MG: 189, 191, 204
  calling of, MG: 115, 116, 118, 152
  history of, is allegory, CH: 74

on sacrifice, TM: 25-27
visions of, MG: 145, 161, 162

Abraham's bosom (see *Abraham, bosom of*)

Abram, MG: 113, 118, 122, 123, 135, 137, 140, 143, 151;
    TM: 25 (see Abraham)

Absolute, the, ASP: 44; CH: 121, 122; JC: 71

abstinence, KL: 4, 140

abundance, MG: 284 (see Prosperity; Supply)
    affirming, P: 41, 71, 93, 108, 120-122, 126, 127, 179,
        186
    all will have, ASP: 16, 17
    consciousness of (see *Consciousness, of Abundance*)
    cultivate ideas of, P: 92, 93, 157
    God's, KL: 101-109, 183, 184; P: 15, 16, 46, 52, 53,
        71, 157, 177
    imagination and, P: 88, 177
    Jabal as symbolizing, MG: 63
    Jesus and, P: 78, 79
    love for God as key to, P: 108-110, 118
    service brings, ASP: 35; P: 9, 150, 151
    Truth affirmations for realizations of, P: 41, 50;
        TP: 41, 83

Accad, (city), MG: 98

accomplishment, ASP: 74

accidents, ASP: 21; CH: 87; TT: 78 (see *chance; luck*)

achievement, TM: 131

acknowledgment, JC: 109

acorn, JC: 28

acquisitiveness, CH: 74, 113, 128; MG: 58, 237; P: 127,

128 (see *Judah; Judas*)

act, CH: 40, 50; MJ: 11, 124

action, P: 26, 58, 59, 92; MJ: 11 (1)
  and reaction, KL: 64; CH: 50 (4)

Acts, ASP: 30, 41; JC: 166; TM: 77, 78; TP: 82

acts, JC: 16, 54; TP: 73, 110; TT: 9, 86, 144
  all involve mind, ideas, and expression, JC: 54
  place them under divine law, JC: 121
  we shall have to square our, JC: 36

Adah, wife of Lamech, MG: 63, 64
  daughter of Elon, MG: 277

Adam, JC: 4, 158; MG: 28, 33, 41, 42, 55-57,
    78; P: 33, 72; TM: 54, 57, 79, 81, 99, 100; TT: 21,
    22, 23, 136, 137
  and Eve, CH: 112; JC: 177, 178; MG: 56;
    TM: 35, 37, 41, 43, 57; TP: 52
  all are included in his sin, KL: 98
  ejected from Eden, KL: 74
  Jesus Christ as, TT: 137
  man, MJ: 12, 13, 36, 37, 61,
    123, 181, 182; TM: 35, 104, 153; TP: 68, 97
    method of generation, KL: 93
    vs. Christ, ASP: 116, 119, 142; MJ: 123
    story of, as allegory or symbolism, CH: 31, 33, 34,
    55-57, 112; JC: 177, 178; KL: 130, 131; MG: 52,
    67, 69; TM: 41, 57, 81; TP: 97; TT: 14-16, 36, 146,
    151

Adamic Consciousness (see *Consciousness, Adamic*)

Adamic man (see *man, Adamic*)

Adamic race (see *race, Adamic*)

Abdeel, MG: 206

desire is, CH: 52, 53
effect of, on mind and body, JC: 13, 14, 192, 193;
TM: 38, 128
faith and, JC: 103, 109; P: 83, 85; TM: 18
formation of Christ Mind in man accelerated by use of,
ASP: 24, 37, 74, 75, 101, 103, 104; TP: 138, 139
given by Jesus, TT: 25, 171
importance of, P: 88, 89, 98, 99, 157, 158, 175, 176,
178, 179
in the name of Christ, ASP: 82; TP: 22, 23
judgment and, ASP: 45-47; CH: 125, 126
justice and, JC: 176
life and, CH: 47; KL: 98; TT: 148-150, 152-154 (see
life, affirmation for more)
Lord's Prayer is, JC: 109; P: 113
love and, MJ: 180
man dominates nature by, ASP: 61
mastering worry, disease, and inharmony by denial and,
ASP: 71, 72
misuse of, CH: 52, 53; TM: 108
of abundance, P: 41
of health, CH: 115; JC: 13, 14, 137, 159, 165, 169,
173, 178, 179, 186
of illumination, P: 35, 36
of one's inheritance from God, ASP: 76
of praise and thanksgiving, JC: 137
of substance, P: 41, 50
of success, P: 54
order and, ASP: 71; JC: 118, 121; P: 111
plenty and, P: 41
prayer is, JC: 67, 70
prosperity and, KL: 107; P: 93, 157
purpose of, KL: 168, 177, 178; P: 56
salvation and, P: 180
strength of, ASP: 50
Truth established in consciousness through, KL: 143
use both denial and, CH: 57; JC: 129
why sometimes not effective, TT: 85, 98
will and, CH: 111, 112, 115

affirmations, CH: 29, 38, 106, 132; JC: 32, 34, 97, 118,

Akan, MG: 287

alah, JC: 141

alcohol, ASP: 21

alert, P: 92

Alexander, TM: 67

allegory, CH: 31, 73, 74, 123; JC: 140, 141, 152, 177,
    178
  definition of, MG: 231
  examples of, ASP: 34, 150; CH: 31, 74; JC: 140, 141,
    152, 177, 178; KL: 130, 131; MG: 9, 11, 24, 34, 44,
    45, 47, 58, 68, 109, 148, 149, 210, 216-218, 220,
    371, 374; TT: 16, 36, 114, 146, 151
  history of Abraham is, CH: 74
  Paul on, CH: 31, 73, 74

All-Good, MG: 284; KL: 33

Allon-bacuth (burial place), MG: 105, 271, 272

all-Presence, CH: 67

all-sufficiency, KL: 102, 103; P: 15, 16, 22

Almightiness, TP: 28

Almighty, the, CH: 8; MG: 150

Almodad, MG: 105

altar, MG: 84, 265, 271; P: 44, 109; TP: 145
  as place in consciousness, KL: 16, 145, 146
  of Jacob, KL: 83
  to an unknown god, KL: 146

Alvah, MG: 291

Alvan, MG: 285

Amalek, MG: 280

Amalekites, MG: 133

ambition, ASP: 36, 172; CH: 53, 54; JC: 100; KL: 59,
    175; MG: 98, 259, 363; MJ: 38, 39; P: 17; TP: 7,
    149, 159; TT: 20

America, MJ: 126

American Standard Version, TM: 44

Ammonites, MG: 170

Amorites, MG: 101, 135, 364

Amraphel, MG: 129

Anah, MG: 284, 286

Anamin, MG: 99, 100

Ananias, P: 164; TM: 75, 76; TT: 126, 127

ancestors, KL: 64, 66, 113; MJ: 89, 90

ancestry, TP: 183-188

Andrew, KL: 117; MG: 238; MJ: 20, 21, 68, 69, 119;
    TM: 16, 18, 34, 45; TT: 53, 91 (see *strength,
    Andrew as representing*)

Aner, MG: 135

Angel of the Lord, TM: 123

angels, ASP: 45-47, 97, 146; CH: 101, 102; JC: 70-72,
    152; KL: 155; MG: 165-167, 228, 255; MJ: 23, 168;
    P: 44-45, 94, (see *ideas*)

anger, CH: 137; JC: 21, 34, 53, 177; KL: 65, 142; TP: 154, 178; TT: 57, 86, 152

animal, KL: 43; MG: 30, 84, 85, 245; TM: 78-82; TP: 26; TT: 59
  as food, TM: 78, 79
  as representing thought, TM: 81, 122
  consciousness (see *consciousness, animal*)
  forces, P: 97, (see *mind, animal forces of*)
  instinct, P: 72
  nature of man, KL: 54, 55, 58-60, 189; MG: 347
  soul, JC: 42; MG: 148, 217; TP: 48, 127

Annas, MJ: 154

anointed one, KL: 10, 15

anointing, MJ: 115, 116; TM: 59

answers (see *prayer, answers to*)

antagonism, TP: 109

anthropology, TP: 67

Antigonus, in "Winter's Tale," ASP: 112

anxiety, ASP: 71, 102; JC: 177; P: 85, 86, 91, 107; TP: 179
  denial of, P: 130

Aorist, first, KL: 109

Apollo, temple of, KL: 38

apostles, ASP: 22, 28, 40; KL: 12, 112, 113, 117 (see *disciples*)

appearances, CH: 93; P: 39, 48, 81, 88, 147; TP: 120
  judging by, ASP: 88; CH: 9, 14; P: 39, 48, 170; TT: 23

not always error, CH: 100

appetite,
  affected by emotions, JC: 53
  repression vs. redemption of, ASP: 72, 73; TM: 155,
    156
  spiritual conquest of, ASP: 20; CH: 115; JC: 130;
    KL: 123; MG: 53; MJ: 51; P: 20, 82; TM: 68, 69,
    168, 169; TP: 105

appropriation, CH: 108, 111; KL: 12, 57, 58, 72, 102,
    122-126, 134, 142, 166, 167, 169, 192, 193;
    MG: 116; MJ: 51, 56, 123, 124; P: 15, 71, 75, 78,
    81, 176; TM: 57, 58, 174; TP: 27, 28, 65, 75, 131;
    TT: 146 (see *substance, appropriation of*)
  of life (see *life, appropriation of*)
  of words, ASP: 78

Aram, MG: 103, 104, 272

Aran, MG: 288

Ararat (mountain), MG: 81, 82

archers, MG: 370

Architect, Great, ASP: 18

Ard, MG: 350

Areli, MG: 347

Arimathea, KL: 195, 196

Arioch, king of Ellasard, MG: 129

ark, MG: 77, 78

Arkite, MG: 101

armor, P: 183, 184

army, Christian, JC: 193, 194

Arnold, Sir Edward (quoted), TT: 27

Arodi, or Arod, MG: 347

Arpachshad, MG: 103

arrogance, TP: 186

arrows, P: 98

arteries, hardening of, TM: 103, 145

artist, the, TM: 101

Arvadite, MG: 101, 102

ascension, ASP: 40, 41; JC: 73, 83, 84; KL: 26, 162;
    MG: 71; MJ: 167

asceticism, TM: 152-153

Asenath, MG: 319, 348; TM: 100-101

Ashbel, MG: 349

Asher, MG: 239, 240, 275, 276, 347, 369

ashes, KL: 138

Ashkenaz, MG: 94

Ashteroth-karnaim (city), MG: 131, 132

Ash Wednesday, KL: 138, 141

asking, CH: 77; JC: 68; MJ: 132; P: 93, 94, 187;
    TM: 93; TP: 169 (see *money, asking for*)
  as first step in attainment of spiritual consciousness,
    TP: 93

by affirmation, JC: 180, 181; TP: 122, 123
for specific things, CH: 69; P: 101
in Jesus' name, CH: 81; TP: 122, 123
in name of Christ (see *Christ, asking and receiving in name of*)

ass, KL: 189; MG: 367

Asshur, MG: 103

Asshurim, MG: 202, 203

Assyria, MG: 37, 38, 98
as psychic realm, ASP: 54, 55

astrology, MG: 103
and Shakespeare, ASP: 113, 114

astronomy, higher, ASP: 161, 162

Atad (threshing floor), MG: 373

"A thief and a robber," MJ: 100

Atlantis, TM: 149, 150

atom, ASP: 11, 16; CH: 44, 62, 65; JC: 21, 41, 44, 145, 146, 149, 174; KL: 28, 38, 39, 69, 132, 179; MJ: 69, 174, 181; P: 10, 33, 48, 179; TM: 4, 5, 54; TP: 60, 98, 109; TT: 33
and its law of expression, ASP: 9, 10, 11, 92
faith center in each, ASP: 40
wisdom at center of, ASP: 92

atomic,
age, ASP: 20
bomb (see *bomb, atomic*)
effects of, on Japanese cities, ASP: 65, 66
spiritual or mental character of, ASP: 12, 13
energy, ASP: 12, 13, 15, 17, 50, 52, 65; MG: 368
power (see *power, atomic*)

structure of universe, ASP: 56

atonement (see *at-one-ment*)
    and race consciousness, TT: 164-166
    Jesus Christ's, KL: 185, 186; TP: 65; TT: 161-178
    meaning of, TT: 164, 165
    vicarious, TT: 167

at-one-ment, JC: 40; KL: 53; MJ: 129, 149; P: 35;
    TP: 65 (see *atonement*)

attainment, ASP: 24; KL: 35, 167; MJ: 74, 75; TT: 99,
    100, 127

attention, MG: 116, 117; TP: 31 (see *concentration*)

attitude, P: 82
    correct mental, CH: 93; JC: 138; KL: 34; TP: 92, 174
    money and, CH: 89, 90
    positive, ASP: 71, 72, 75

attraction, TP: 108
    law of, ASP: 72

attributes, (see *faculties*)
    divine, ASP: 46, 49, 151
    of God, TM: 131, 132, 145, 163
    of mind, TM: 145

aura, TP: 61, 123
    of body, ASP: 158
    of soul, ASP: 157; JC: 138, 139
    spiritual, JC: 76, 110, 138, 139, 146

authority, ASP: 47; MG: 220, 318; TP: 141
    and bondage, TT: 92, 104
    given to every child of God, JC: 178, 186; P: 47, 160,
      161; TP: 28, 88
    of Jesus, KL: 29, 72, 73; TP: 165

avarice, CH: 52, 53; P: 127, 128, 148, 153, 156, 157, 167;

B

Baal, MG: 290, 349

Baalhanan, MG: 290

Babel, city and tower, MG: 98, 108-111

Babylon, king of, ASP: 19

back, TM: 18, 19

Bacon, Lord Francis, ASP: 108

bacteriology, TM: 148

balance, MG: 23, 70, 97, 376; P: 150, 170; TT: 29, 58
  law of universal, KL: 43

ballast, TT: 29

baptism, TP: 67, 68 (see *Holy Spirit*)
  as cleansing of denial, MJ: 17-19, 35, 41-43, 110;
    TM: 19, 150
  by water, TM: 150, 151
  Christ, gives infusion of power, KL: 73; TM: 18
  Holy Spirit, ASP: 28, 30, 31, 66, 67, 130; CH: 28, 58;
    MJ: 181, 182; TM: 61, 88, 89, 90, 154; TT: 73, 90,
    91, 106, 107, 151
  of fire, TT: 151
  of Jesus (see *Jesus, baptism of*)
  prayer treatment as, ASP: 67
  Pentecostal, JC: 194
  Spirit, ASP: 130
  spiritual, ASP: 27, 28, 66, 67; JC: 194; TP: 162, 163

Barabbas, MJ: 158

19

bargaining, P: 151

Barnabas, P: 164

barren, MG: 278, 285, 286

barriers, thoughts as, JC: 33

Bartholomew, MJ: 21-23; TM: 16, 20-21, 72

Basemath, MG: 217, 218, 277

battery, electric, JC: 14

battle, MG: 265

bear, P: 184

Beasley, Norman ("Let's Operate"), TP: 104, 105

beast, MG: 24, 40, 42; TP: 97
  of the field, P: 97; TM: 22, 79, 81, 161, 169; TT: 15, 16

beauty, MG: 63, 64, 201, 277; P: 57, 94
  soul's delight in, MG: 186, 200, 208, 271

Becher, MG: 349

Beecher, Lyman, TM: 144

Beeri, MG: 217, 218

Beer-lahai-roi, MG: 149, 200, 205

Beer-sheba (place), MG: 179-181, 185, 217, 341

Beethoven and the "inner ear," TP: 117

beggar, MJ: 96-98; TT: 156

begging, TP: 28, 35, 159

beginning, KL: 46

"Behold the Angel," (Morgan), ASP: 23, 24

beholding, KL: 44

Being, CH: 34; JC: 151; KL: 132, 133; MJ: 28, 69, 136;
    P: 14, 32, 75; TP: 24, 159; TT: 29, 30, 32, 33, 43,
    153, 158, 161
  and expression, ASP: 138; CH: 55; JC: 131, 133, 177;
    P: 27-29
  and Jesus, ASP: 38, 41; TT: 164, 165, 169
  as aggregation of ideas, JC: 177
  as always present, CH: 66, 67
  as both masculine and feminine, TM: 53
  as Christ, JC: 148
  as impersonal principle, CH: 34; MJ: 76
  as Jehovah God, JC: 158; TT: 14, 15
  as Principle and person, TP: 168, 169
  attributes of (see *Being, character of*)
  cause and effect as law of, TT: 78
  character of, ASP: 134; CH: 7-16; JC: 24, 29, 141,
    165; KL: 58; MJ: 19; TM: 52, 53; TP: 11; TT: 14,
    42, 55, 64, 157
  consciousness of our life in, JC: 165
  defined, JC: 24; P: 14
  demonstration and, P: 37
  desire and fulfillment as principle of, TT: 79
  equilibrium of, KL: 43; TT: 58, 59
  freedom is essential part of, CH: 112
  how to stir powers of, JC: 18, 19
  law of unfoldment in, KL: 88; TT: 24, 25
  life is inherent in, TT: 40
  logic of, CH: 10; JC: 190, 191
  man is, in miniature, CH: 42; KL: 54
  pleasure as an end contrary to law of, TM: 57
  powers of, KL: 54, 55, 170; TT: 136
  science of, CH: 7, 14
  spiritual character as foundation of, MJ: 122

spiritual man and, KL: 88; MG: 116, 117; TM: 54
Truth of, CH: 10, 55
unchanging laws of, JC: 34, 59, 84, 177
universal intelligence of, KL: 49
will and understanding cannot be divorced from,
    CH: 108
wisdom and love as expressive and receptive side of,
    MG: 27
word of, CH: 61; MJ: 11

be-ing, pure, KL: 170

Bela,
    king of Edom, MG: 289
    son of Benjamin, MG: 349

belief, JC: 99, 113, 133; KL: 76; P: 49; TT: 167
    all things are possible if we have, CH: 92; JC: 138;
        KL: 38, 76; TM: 32; TT: 49
    in negation, ASP: 76, 119; KL: 5, 48, 49, 66, 67;
        TT: 45
    is form of faith, CH: 85, 86
    is made manifest through power of the word, KL: 17;
        TT: 143, 144, 166
    opens the way for entrance of Spirit, KL: 57; P: 48

believers, signs that accompany, JC: 79

Bellamy, Edward ("Looking Backward"), ASP: 31, 32

Ben-ammi, MG: 170

Benjamin, MG: 236, 273, 275, 327, 328, 330, 331-334,
    335-337, 340, 349, 350, 370 (see *faith*)

Bera, MG: 130, 136, 137

Bered (place), MG: 149

Beriah, MG: 347

22

Bethany, MJ: 109, 110, 115

Bethel, or Luz (town), MG: 120, 123, 229, 248, 270, 271, 359, 360

Bethesda, Pool of, JC: 96; MJ: 57

Bethlehem, or Ephrath, MG: 273; TP: 49

Bethsaida, MJ: 21

Bethuel, MG: 186, 199, 208, 226

betrayal, MJ: 116, 117, 128

Bhakti (Disciples of Love), TT: 59

Bible, ASP: 18, 20, 24, 63; MG: 44;
    MJ: 53; P: 62; TM: 63, 90; TP: 62, 101, 120;
    KL: 97
  analysis of, not sacrilegious, ASP: 84
  and evolution, TP: 66, 67
  and miracles, ASP: 54, 83, 84
  and overcoming, P: 96, 97
  as allegorical record of man, ASP: 80, 116; CH: 31,
    72-74, 123; MG: 10, 11, 159, 163, 231, 371;
    TP: 140
  as Book of Life, P: 180
  as exposition of human mind and body, CH: 73, 74
  as guide to spiritual unfoldment, MG: 10, 11, 293
  as textbook of Absolute Truth, ASP: 162, 163
  as textbook on redemption of man, ASP: 103
  bears witness of Savior, MJ: 66
  characters represent ideas, P: 50, 70, 179, 180 (see
    Bible, as allegorical record of man)
  Glossary of Antiquities (quoted), CH: 119
  interpretation of, ASP: 162, 170; KL: 97; MG: 10-13,
    22, 293, 371
  is it sole word of God?, ASP: 127, 129; MG: 44
  key to, JC: 71, 139
  man and his states of mind represented in, ASP: 80

mysticism and inspiration of, JC: 139, 141
not sufficient to impart spiritual understanding, MJ: 65,
    66
on "brain of the heart," TM: 90
on death, ASP: 142
on physiology, TM: 40
paramount theme of, ASP: 116
plenty prophesied in, TT: 122
Scofield translation of, MG: 150
symbolism of, CH: 72
translation of, ASP: 162, 170; TP: 3
vs. living Word, MJ: 65, 66

Bilhah, MG: 235, 237, 238, 240, 274, 294

Bilhan, MG: 287

bills, P: 120, 125, 177

bind, KL: 117, 118
binding, P: 176, 177

bird, MG: 22, 40; TP: 55

birds of the heavens, TT: 15, 16

Birsha, MG: 130

birth, TM: 138, 172
  and rebirth, TM: 138; TT: 75-78, 88
  first, CH: 25, 26, 73
  new, CH: 25, 26, 28; JC: 52, 85; KL: 162; MG: 174,
    175, 177; MJ: 33, 34, 35, 37, 38, 82; P: 179;
    TM: 80
  physical, TT: 75-77, 84, 89, 90
  second, CH: 25, 26
  spiritual, TT: 75-88, 90

birthright, MG: 209-211; P: 87

Blackstone, P: 59

24

through)

as dynamo, JC: 14; MJ: 174

as formed in the regeneration, ASP: 42, 43, 119

as Garden of Eden, KL: 147; MG: 52; TM: 163, 167, 168

as house, MG: 228, 229, 260; MJ: 88

as ideas in Divine Mind, KL: 167; TT: 117-119

as important part of man, KL: 81, 82, 93, 96

as innately spiritual, MG: 177, 292

as instrument of mind, ASP: 20, 43, 71, 75, 80, 81, 119-121, 133, 146, 147, 149, 169; KL: 81, 82, 118; MG: 99; TT: 32, 62, 63, 106, 107, 116, 117, 119, 147-160 (see *body is moved and built by thought; thought, as director of body forces*)

as man's universe, JC: 161

as perfect creation, KL: 10, 11, 13, 19, 22, 167; TT: 93, 117, 118 (see *I AM, and perfect*)

as potentially eternal (immortal), ASP: 24, 25, 66, 120, 121, 122, 131, 142; JC: 111; KL: 21, 68, 69, 95, 151, 162, 163; MJ: 96, 97, 110, 172-174; TM: 23, 91, 171, 172, 174; TP: 6, 67, 79, 94, 128; TT: 112, 113, 146-160

as precipitation of man's soul, TP: 109, 110

as projection of man's ideas, CH: 34, 40, 43, 45, 52, 99, 105; JC: 186

as record of man's thoughts, ASP: 70, 116, 118, 119, 121, 122; TT: 116

as representative of sum of animal world, TM: 79, 81, 82

as result of our millions of years of labor, KL: 52, 130

as self-renewing, CH: 41; KL: 98, 167; TT: 115, 116

as temple of living God, ASP: 70, 80, 81, 116, 118, 119, 121, 122, 144, 145; JC: 64, 175, 185; KL: 21, 22, 146, 167, 168, 182; MG: 260; MJ: 28, 29, 31, 32, 96, 97; TM: 25, 135; TP: 128; TT: 90, 105-108, 118-121 (see *blessing, of body temple*)

of Holy Spirit, ASP: 117, 131

astral, ASP: 146

as transformer of life, TT: 41, 42, 63

attainment of perfection in, KL: 95, 96, 98, 99, 166-168

transfiguration of, ASP: 153, 157
transformation of, JC: 40-42, 63, 71, 163, 184;
    KL: 168; MJ: 173, 174, 181; TT: 62, 63, 107, 108,
    111-113; 153
Truth statements for healing and regenerating, CH: 52;
    JC: 64-66; MG: 122
union of mind and, MG: 262, 263
vs. ideal, JC: 51, 52, 66, 184
vs. mind, MG: 224, 225
weakness of, CH: 54
we must bless the, (see *blessing of body temple*)

boll weevil, P: 139

bomb, ASP: 29
  atomic, ASP: 12, 13, 15, 17, 50, 52, 56, 65, 66;
    KL: 41, 42

bondage, ASP: 78; JC: 60; KL: 127, 128, 180; MG: 313;
    MJ: 28; TM: 103, 116, 122, 124-127, 129; TT: 104,
    164, 166

bone, MJ: 164

book of life, JC: 20; P: 180; TM: 63

Book of Moses, MJ: 65

books, TT: 140
  of physical science, JC: 142

"born anew," MJ: 33, 35; TP: 15, 24

bounty, P: 24, 96, 134

bow, MG: 364

bowels, TM: 21, 144, 158, 159

Brahma, CH: 10

brain, ASP: 51; CH: 96, 131; MG: 127; TM: 90 (see *mind*)
  as seat of telepathy, TP: 154
  cells (see *cells, brain*)
  center (see *center, brain*)
  evolved by mind, ASP: 34; TP: 79
  faith and man's, ASP: 125
  front, CH: 99, 100
    as seat of understanding, MJ: 171; TM: 16, 21
    as seat of imagination, TM: 16, 20, 71
    as seat of will, MJ: 162, 171; TM: 16, 21, 22, 100, 101
  of the heart, TM: 90
  radiates beams when we think, ASP: 83; KL: 38
  testers, TP: 91
  upper, CH: 86
  voltage, ASP: 30

branch, MJ: 137

bread, KL: 192
  and fish, MJ: 177, 178
  and wine, ASP: 77; JC: 144, 145, 158, 159; KL: 133, 166, 167, 192, 313; MG: 136
  as universal substance, MG: 136, 313, 369; MJ: 115, 178; P: 31, 80, 81, 95, 96, 164, 165
  eating, meaning of, MG: 158, 253
    breaking, P: 71
  Jesus as, ASP: 31, 77; KL: 133, 166, 167, 192
  man does not live by, alone, ASP: 137; MJ: 180

breakdown, nervous, MG: 76

breast, TM: 62

breastplate, CH: 120; TM: 47

breath, ASP: 15; MG: 34, 37, 58
  of God, CH: 8; KL: 17; MJ: 19, 136; TT: 134
  of life, CH: 33
  of Spirit, CH: 8

of the Almighty, CH: 7

breathing, TM: 54; TT: 147, 148
  "threatening and slaughter," ASP: 26

broadcasting stations, ASP: 16

brother, MG: 335

brotherhood, MG: 350; P: 136, 143
  Jesus recognized, KL: 32
  universal, CH: 131, 132; JC: 62; KL: 32; P: 143;
    TT: 8

brothers, five, TT: 157, 158

Browning, Elizabeth Barrett (quoted), TP: 11

Browning, Robert (quoted), ASP: 18; TP: 16

Brutus, in "Julius Caesar," ASP: 114

Bryant, William Cullen ("Thanatopsis"), TT: 48

builder, man as, ASP: 121, 139; KL: 46; TT: 16, 90, 92

burdens, KL: 52, 53; MG: 367; TM: 19; TP: 110, 111;
    TT: 94, 95, 111, 127
  mental, MG: 266, 267, 297; P: 122-125, 129, 172;
    TP: 23

burial, MG: 358, 376

bush, TM: 122, 123

business, P: 156, 157; TM: 15
  and good judgment, CH: 127, 128
  and praise, CH: 79
  and proper attitude toward money, KL: 102-107
  and tithing, KL: 84, 85, 86
  cause of depression in, P: 167, 168, 171

C

Caesar, ASP: 109, 110, 114, 128; MJ: 161, 162

Caiaphas, MJ: 155

Cain (body), MG: 58, 60-65, 70

Calah, MG: 99

call, divine, MG: 118

called, the, ASP: 33, 34

Calneh (city), MG: 98

Calpurnia, in "Julius Caesar," ASP: 109-111

Calvary, "place of a skull," KL: 194, 195

Cana, MJ: 24-26; "place of reeds," KL: 75; TM: 141

Canaan,
  as representing mind, MG: 96
  son of Ham, MG: 84, 85, 89, 90, 96, 266, 284
  land of, 102, 120, 126, 144, 146, 152, 153, 248, 264,
    265, 269, 273, 276, 277, 324, 325, 339, 341, 342,
    353, 354, 376; TM: 120, 124, 134

Canaanites, MG: 146, 269, 306, 373; P: 156

cancer, TM: 145

candlestick, TP: 153

Capernaum, MJ: 28, 73

Caphtorium, MG: 100

capital, ASP: 172

captives, P: 74

Cardiac plexus, as love center, KL: 34; (see *plexus, cardiac*)
    See also Heart

carelessness, ASP: 75; P: 111

cares, KL: 52, 53

Carlyle, Thomas, ASP: 156; TP: 21, 25

Carmi, MG: 344

carnal, (see *mind, carnal*)

carpenter, KL: 116

Carrel, Dr. Alexis (quoted), TP: 79

Casluhim, MG: 100

Cassius, in "Julius Caesar," ASP: 114

catarrh, TT: 154

cattle, MG: 24, 40, 354

Cause, CH: 10, 13, 16; P: 93

cause, ASP: 134; TP: 178; TT: 8-10, 18, 19, 162 (see
    Mind, as underlying cause)
    and effect, ASP: 104, 135, 140, 160; CH: 8-10, 80, 81,
        93, 101, 107, 113; JC: 5, 16, 22, 30, 44, 49, 53, 57,
        58, 69, 84, 92, 112, 123, 127, 132, 136, 190; KL: 14,
        46, 88; MG: 8, 9, 107, 351; P: 18, 39, 40, 58, 88, 97,
        103, 146, 147, 150, 154, 170; TM: 139; TP: 34, 73,
        74, 98; TT: 32, 33, 44, 45, 48, 78, 80, 82, 113, 162
    the one, KL: 63
    thought as, (see *thought, as cause*)

cave, MG: 19, 192

cells, CH: 135; P: 72, 79; TM: 37, 54, 128
  and ideas, CH: 44, 45, 99; JC: 40, 41, 72, 75
  and passions, JC: 130, 176
  and thought, ASP: 147, 148; CH: 52, 74, 75; JC: 73,
    127, 146, 170, 172, 192; KL: 20, 38, 39; TM: 146
  and words, CH: 136, 137; JC: 186; KL: 20; TP: 82
  as affected by consciousness, JC: 12, 13, 77, 169;
    KL: 186, 187; TM: 19; TT: 49, 50, 153, 154
  as electric batteries, JC: 14, 185
  as units of light and energy, TP: 60, 61, 79
  body, as centers of force, ASP: 24; JC: 73, 138, 146,
    147, 160, 161, 172, 192
  brain, ASP: 14, 15, 30, 84; CH: 79, 86, 87, 96, 97;
    JC: 46, 73, 160; TP: 59, 91
  can develop independent power of seeing and hearing,
    ASP: 56, 57; P: 175
  contain record of our experiences since beginning,
    ASP: 70
  electronic energy is imprisoned in body, ASP: 13, 14,
    41; KL: 132; TM: 5
  how created, JC: 44, 45
  live vs. dead, JC: 12, 13; TT: 152
  of body of Jesus, ASP: 22, 40, 169; JC: 11, 41, 72,
    146, 194
  of body of Jesus Christ, JC: 194, 195
  transformation of, ASP: 14, 22, 24, 25, 66, 157, 158;
    JC: 41, 52, 72, 163, 192; TP: 66, 68

center,
  brain, CH: 63, 64, 74, 75, 86, 87, 97, 109; TM: 22, 37,
    102, 140; TP: 117, 127
  faith, CH: 86
  ganglionic, CH: 75; MG: 231; TM: 16, 134
  generative, CH: 46; TM: 22, 147, 161-174
  life, CH: 46, 47; KL: 123; MG: 217, 306; TM: 162,
    163
  love, CH: 38, 130; KL: 34; P: 102; TM: 91; TT: 62,
    63, 64, 65
  nerve, CH: 74, 75, 97, 100; TM: 18-20, 37, 49, 102,

charm, good luck, CH: 87

chastity, MG: 269

Chedorlaomer, king of Elam, MG: 129, 133, 134

cheerfulness,
   as aid to healing, TP: 104-106, 132-134
   as promoter of prosperity, TP: 104-106 (see *giver, God*
     loves a cheerful) See also Health
   as step in fulfillment of law, P: 92
   in giving, P: 152, 158

chemicalization, MG: 71

chemistry, P: 77

Cheran, MG: 286, 287

Cherubim, MG: 57

Chesed, MG: 186

Chezib (town), MG: 303, 304

chief captain, MJ: 154

chief priests, MJ: 82, 83, 152

child,
   and imagination, P: 81, 82
   and pressure, TM: 159
   disobedience in, TM: 108
   is naturally happy, KL: 107, 108
   of God, ASP: 27, 167 (see *man, as child of God*)
   reacts to words, CH: 65, 78, 79
   symbolism of, MG: 29; P: 113
   training, CH: 109; TM: 105

children, relation to the kingdom, KL: 107

Children of Israel, ASP: 82, 83; TT: 137
  and making a living, KL: 106
  and Pharaoh, TM: 122, 123, 128, 129
  enslavement of, MG: 144, 145
  symbolism of, ASP: 143; MG: 178, 374; MJ: 75, 96,
    97; P: 71, 156, 180; TM: 24, 25, 89, 103, 121,
    126-129

China, MJ: 126; P: 90

Chinese, JC: 90; TT: 173

choosing, ASP: 78, 119

chosen,
  of God, ASP: 78; JC: 115, 116; MG: 151

Christ, ASP: 30, 80, 171, 172; CH: 126; JC: 135, 145,
    150; KL: 15, 16, 25, 27, 117, 118, 140, 174, 194;
    MJ: 12, 59, 71, 82, 105, 112, 136, 170; TM: 70;
    TP: 52; TT: 34, 35, 50, 134, 167, 169, 177, (see
    Jesus; Jesus Christ)
  all men are one in, P: 143, 144
  all shall be made alive in, JC: 4
  and atonement, KL: 185
  and fourth dimension, KL: 140
  and His reign in man, TT: 124, 131
  and I AM THAT I AM, MJ: 92
  and prayer, ASP: 30
  and regeneration, TT: 154, 155
  and reincarnation, TP: 149, 150
  and soul, ASP: 151; MJ: 47, 48
  as discerner of thoughts, MJ: 31, 48
  as door into kingdom of God, ASP: 136; TM: 50,
    118-120
  as God's idea of man, KL: 10, 15, 53, 63; MG: 12, 32,
    33; MJ: 61, 62, 64, 76; P: 85
  as higher self, CH: 53; MJ: 17
  as I AM, JC: 157; MJ: 128, 134, 158; P: 93
  as image and likeness, ASP: 100, 101
  as inner principle, CH: 66, 67, 107, 126

calling on strength of, MJ: 70, 71

cannot experience death, MJ: 92

church of, (see *church, of Christ*)

coming of, JC: 149, 150; TM: 15, 68

communing with, ASP: 76, 77, 101; MG: 77, 139

consciousness, ASP: 33, 44, 150, 151, 171, 172; CH: 98, 137, 138; JC: 40, 77, 123; KL: 11, 53, 61, 67, 98, 112, 114, 115, 142, 158, 162, 168, 171; MG: 24, 57, 72, 136, 149, 175, 348; MJ: 47, 82, 84, 85, 88, 102, 114, 149, 170; P: 175, 176; TM: 118, 119, 120; TP: 43, 178; TT: 137, 143, 165, 166, 167, 169, 170

attainment of, TP: 43, 178

defined, JC: 9-11

demonstrating, by thought, ASP: 70-79, 120, 124, 148, 150; TT: 148

distinction between Jesus and, JC: 9, 10

equal to God, MJ: 61, 62

false, JC: 20

Holy Spirit is interpreter of, TT: 141

I AM, JC: 157 (see *I AM, as Christ; as Christ in man*)

incarnations of, KL: 130-133

indwelling, JC: 40, 105, 106, 178; KL: 11, 24-29, 171, 193; MG: 82, 116; MJ: 52, 85, 98, 99

"in you, the hope of glory," ASP: 13, 80; MJ: 14; P: 76

Jehovah as, (see *Jehovah, as Christ*)

Jesus as, ASP: 100, 122; KL: 134; MJ: 41, 80, 84-87, 92, 114, 122, 128, 149, 154, 156; TP: 150

joy and freedom of, MG: 325, 326

life, ASP: 24; JC: 158, 159; MJ: 31, 102, 167

listening to voice of, TP: 117

love of, as cleanser of man's mind, MJ: 127

man, ASP: 130, 131; CH: 23, 107; JC: 9, 10, 11, 28, 131, 132; KL: 28, 53, 63, 95, 110, 111, 113; MG: 25, 26, 30, 33, 34, 65, 159, 207, 208, 364, 365; MJ: 13; TM: 54; TP: 110; TT: 148

man's access to, JC: 17

man's attachment to God through, TP: 12, 13

man's desire to bring forth, MG: 116, 141, 144

man's dominion over psychic realm through, TP: 52, 53

Christianizing all nations, MJ: 169, 170

Christlikeness, MG: 65

Chronicles, JC: 171

church, CH: 37 (see *Church of Christ*)
  and orthodoxy, MJ: 33, 34; TM: 110-118; TT: 132,
    133, 138, 139, 164
  Christian, JC: 79
  defined, KL: 119; MJ: 29, 30
  fathers, and Shakespeare, ASP: 107, 108, 129
  Jesus Christ and, (see *Jesus Christ, and church*)
  of Christ, JC: 102; KL: 115, 160
  of God, KL: 115
  of Jesus Christ, P: 52
  Peter and the, CH: 86; JC: 50; TT: 102, 103

Church of Christ,
  as body of Christ, ASP: 78, 79
  as exact science, TT: 110-111
  as man's spiritual body, TT: 105, 106, 112, 113
  as state of consciousness, TT: 52, 105, 106, 110
  external, compared with minds and hearts of men,
    TT: 109
  whole life of man covered by, TT: 111

circumcision, MG: 153, 154, 156

circumstances, ASP: 82; JC: 35, 36

city, CH: 27, 28

civilization, ASP: 31, 68; JC: 193; MG: 109-111; P: 146,
    148, 149; TT: 124-126

clairvoyance, MJ: 21, 22

Clark, Glenn (quoted), TP: 3

clay, ASP: 19; MJ: 98

Comforter,
    as Holy Spirit, JC: 179, 182, 195; KL: 16, 17, 28;
      MJ: 81, 133, 134, 141, 143; TT: 133
    as Spirit of truth, JC: 179, 195; MJ: 141; TP: 123
    as Spirit of wholeness, JC: 182
    Christ as, KL: 28, 29
    Jesus and, (see *Jesus, and Comforter*)

commerce, P: 128, 147, 156

commandment, the great, KL: 41, 42; TP: 58, 113

commercialism, JC: 151; TP: 128

common sense vs. fanaticism, MJ: 119

communal living, P: 126, 127, 149, 150, 151, 164

communion, (see *prayer; silence; Holy Spirit, as avenue for*
    man's communion with God)
    eating bread as, MG: 253
    with God, ASP: 20, 21, 32, 76; CH: 25, 92; JC: 24, 25,
      32, 33, 57; KL: 5, 51, 58; TP: 43, 160; TT: 71, 72,
      98, 136-138
    with Jesus Christ (see *Jesus Christ, communing with*)
    with the Father, ASP: 21, 94, 95; TM: 115, 116, 117

compensation, MG: 193

competition, TM: 68, 100

competence, P: 92

complexion, CH: 124, 126, 127

conceit, KL: 33, 66

concentration, KL: 120, 121; MG: 117; P: 80 (see *mind,*
    concentration of)
    and realization, JC: 45
    and visualization, P: 84

as mental magnet, JC: 44
equal to prayer, JC: 48, 70; TP: 20, 31, 32, 130
intellectual, ASP: 11, 158; CH: 152; JC: 19, 48, 52;
   KL: 16
of thought, (see *thought, concentration of*)
of will, JC: 188; KL: 11, 12
spiritual, ASP: 29; MJ: 88, 89; P: 41; TP: 81, 131

concept, JC: 133; KL: 24, 132, 133; MJ: 111

condemnation, CH: 93; MJ: 65, 66, 85; TT: 84
   affirmation for overcoming, P: 123
   and damnation, KL: 98
   as a boomerang, CH: 122, 123
   law and, (see *law, and condemnation*)
   of material things, P: 105
   of self, CH: 90, 125
   of sense man, TM: 152, 153
   Paul on, KL: 98
   personal judgment leads to, CH: 122-125
   vs. faith, CH: 89, 90, 93
   vs. love, P: 110, 123, 124

conditions, CH: 92, 93
   external, MJ: 177
   how made, CH: 63, 64, 100; JC: 189
   old, P: 174, 175, 184

confidence,
   in self, ASP: 74; CH: 85, 86; MG: 120
   in Spirit, ASP: 71

conflict, P: 180

Confucius (quoted), MJ: 30

confusion, racial, ASP: 68
   remedy for, JC: 150

congestion, CH: 53; JC: 168, 169; TM: 108; TP: 82, 127

Congress, P: 58

conscience, KL: 43-53; MG: 259, 328
   accusing, how to dissolve, KL: 53
   animals feel its power in them, KL: 43
   as a divine goodness at root of all existence, KL: 43
   as continuous guide for every person, KL: 43, 158
   as law of universal balance, KL: 43
   as voice of Holy Spirit, KL: 43
   as voice of Jehovah, MG: 51, 52
   failure may give, an opportunity, KL: 44
   wants exact justice, KL: 43

conscious mind, (see *mind, conscious*)

consciousness, ASP: 18, 45; CH: 36, 57, 93; JC: 24, 50,
    64, 69, 77, 82, 111, 152; KL: 57, 62; MG: 107;
    MJ: 26, 28, 32, 62, 69, 100, 107, 114, 122, 151, 152,
    165, 180; P: 44, 56, 70, 71, 107, 108, 113; TM: 25,
    38, 65, 72, 105, 124, 132, 142-144, 149-151, 163,
    164; TP: 16, 18, 20, 32, 119, 120, 168, 170; TT: 72,
    80, 106, 115, 117, 118, 124, 125, 130, 158
   Adamic, JC: 40; KL: 60, 61, 98, 130, 131, 171;
    MG: 68, 82; TT: 14, 15
   adverse, MJ: 158
   affected by spiritual forces, TM: 123-128
   altar represents a center of, KL: 145
   and love, CH: 92; JC: 35, 62; KL: 30; MJ: 180;
    P: 173; TP: 113; TT: 60, 72
   and mind, JC: 31, 33, 34
   and praise, JC: 138, 139; KL: 12; MG: 305, 366, 367;
    P: 35, 41, 105, 155; TP: 82, 90, 91
   and soul unfoldment, MJ: 22, 26, 110, 111, 165 (see
    soul, evolution of)
   and thanksgiving, (see *thanksgiving, as means of develop-
    ing spiritual*)
   animal, MG: 58, 63, 68, 99, 100, 132, 215, 278, 286,
    289, 291, 347, 350; TP: 30

evolution of Jesus from sense, ASP: 34, 37

expanded by praise, KL: 12, 107

faith, CH: 87; JC: 101; MG: 175; TP: 32
as foundation of, KL: 114, 115, 117

fall of man is his own, KL: 54

fears in, MG: 97

flesh, KL: 77, 78; TT: 77-88, 96, 107

formed by thought, JC: 33; TT: 54, 71, 106, 152

God's power incorporated in, KL: 124, 143, 147

God's two planes of, MG: 26, 27

heaven and hell as states of, ASP: 97; KL: 116;
TP: 101, 138, 139, 144, 178

high, MG: 81-83, 167, 195, 248; TM: 27

I AM, ASP: 47; JC: 123; KL: 82, 124, 190; MJ: 57,
139; TP: 144; TT: 77 (see *I AM, as center of consciousness*)

ideas—forming into states of, MG: 116, 117, 263

incorporating body of Christ into, MJ: 75

individual, CH: 108, 109; MG: 108, 290

Jacob and his states of, KL: 83

Jerusalem as spiritual center in, MJ: 56

Jesus, ASP: 77, 169; KL: 169; MJ: 49, 147, 173;
TP: 29, 64

Jesus Christ, ASP: 40, 41, 44; MJ: 16, 30; P: 71;
TP: 12, 17, 20, 22, 29, 43, 57, 65, 69; TT: 127, 142,
143, 164-167, 178

Judas, CH: 58, 59, 74; MJ: 116, 117

layers of, in body, KL: 52; TM: 70

making superconsciousness an abiding state of, ASP: 36

manifesting that which is held in, ASP: 48, 72

man's perfected, as God's house or temple, ASP: 94

material, ASP: 155; KL: 83; MG: 96, 101, 102, 189,
280, 291, 292, 355; MJ: 36, 37; TP: 144

mixed state of, MJ: 49, 82

mortal, ASP: 57; KL: 50; TM: 70

new, established by Jesus for the race, KL: 169

of abiding substance, P: 20, 32, 79, 171

of abundance, P: 41, 79, 80, 88, 89, 96, 100, 113, 120,
127, 156, 166, 182

of divine supply, (see *supply, consciousness of divine*)

of eternal life, ASP: 151; KL: 100

50

of God, TT: 15, 136
  as one's resource, TP: 89
of God's love, P: 103, 122, 123
of God's presence, MG: 260
of good and evil, TM: 42, 43
of health, ASP: 77; JC: 23, 40, 44, 46, 123; P: 122,
  123
of I AM presence, JC: 123, 135
of inherent wisdom, ASP: 77
of Jesus, (see *Jesus, consciousness of*)
of kingdom of heaven, P: 38, 141, 142
of lack, P: 62, 168, 169 (see *consciousness, of poverty*)
of life, JC: 17, 64, 94, 103-105; KL: 122, 123, 163;
  MG: 61, 305; TM: 22, 158, 161; TT: 148
of limitation, P: 52
of nakedness and separation from God, KL: 54
of peace, JC: 21, 176, 177
of poverty, P: 90, 98 (see *consciousness, of lack*)
of prosperity, ASP: 57; KL: 103; MJ: 68, 69; P: 68,
  69, 90, 100, 101, 124, 125, 128, 129; TP: 122, 123;
  TT: 55
of separation from God, TT: 15
of sin, TT: 154
of spiritual origin, KL: 65
of spiritual substance, MJ: 74; P: 78, 79, 117, 171
of union with Source, JC: 146
perfected through thought, KL: 16-18, 64, 65, 113-116
personal, ASP: 40, 41; CH: 15, 59, 97, 98, 116;
  JC: 10, 98; KL: 94, 95; MG: 367; TM: 70, 124,
  172; TT: 14, 157, 169, 177
planes of, three, MG: 84, 85
power of Word and, KL: 15, 17
power of words on, CH: 137; JC: 99; KL: 17, 168;
  TM: 63
prayer awakens spiritual, ASP: 32, 33
primitive relation to cause, KL: 68
psychic, JC: 51
purification of, P: 157
race, ASP: 29, 39, 142; CH: 24, 25, 35; JC: 4, 30, 146,
  147, 159, 184; KL: 74, 75, 96, 113, 131, 181, 185;
  MJ: 63; P: 127-128, 150-153; TP: 22, 50, 64, 65,

51

68, 69, 183-188; TT: 45, 46, 61, 123-125, 164, 168
(see *Jesus, and race consciousness*)
    and avarice, P: 127, 128
    and charity, P: 152, 153
    and money, P: 150, 151
resting in Spirit, KL: 70
results from thinking, KL: 65, 114, 165
salvation dependent on, KL: 115; MJ: 49; TM: 118,
    119; TT: 118, 119
Satanic, KL: 107
sense, ASP: 93-95, 170; CH: 15; JC: 89; KL: 60, 96,
    130, 171, 196; MG: 24, 35, 46-49, 54, 55, 63, 71, 88,
    89, 97, 101, 106, 113, 115, 124, 125, 131-133, 138,
    161-163, 180, 183, 187, 207, 213, 258, 288, 299,
    308, 310, 339, 350, 353; MJ: 48, 57, 68, 69, 89, 116,
    117, 119, 161; TM: 102, 120, 167; TP: 11, 52, 119;
    TT: 62, 79, 110, 156, 158, 159, 161, 164, 172
    vs. spiritual, TM: 56, 57, 120, 121, 124, 125
separating the erroneous from the true in, ASP: 49
shattering man's fixed states of, by spoken word,
    ASP: 54, 55
six steps in formation of, TP: 182
Son-of-God, TM: 6, 44, 50, 89
soul as, ASP: 151; MG: 34
spiritual, ASP: 28, 53, 57, 157, 169; CH: 66, 75, 87,
    131; JC: 86, 159, 172, 173, 180; KL: 58, 70, 77, 78,
    88, 148, 192, 193; MG: 56, 57, 85, 88, 123, 165,
    171, 194, 215, 231, 264, 303, 311; MJ: 17, 19, 41,
    119, 125-127, 162, 163; P: 9, 48, 109; TM: 6, 7, 38,
    39, 93, 99, 120, 125, 135, 151, 152, 157; TP: 48;
    TT: 33, 72-74, 77, 88, 89, 127, 164, 168
    vs. material, P: 175, 176
strata of, have been built through ages, KL: 52
thinking faculty as executive power in, TT: 54
thoughts manifested as states of, ASP: 48, 76, 94, 95
three great factors in, TM: 164
true church of Christ as state of, TT: 105, 106, 110
Truth statement for realization of higher, KL: 77, 78,
    98, 99, 107; MG: 320
two planes of, KL: 176
universal, KL: 100

Cornelius, TM: 78

cosmic ether, ASP: 40

cotton, P: 139

coughing, TT: 154

country, KL: 83; TP: 144
  another, TT: 54
  far, TT: 99
  new, MG: 115, 127; TT: 85

courage, ASP: 39; CH: 138; KL: 36-42; MG: 257;
  P: 124, 144 (see *love*)

covenant, JC: 116; KL: 84; MG: 85, 86, 123, 124, 155,
  158, 159, 181, 211; P: 20; TP: 145, 146; TT: 84, 85

covetousness, P: 123, 142, 149-151, 154; TP: 154
  as hindrance to successful community life, P: 148, 149,
  151

creation, CH: 35; JC: 4, 16; KL: 54, 61
  accomplished through power of word, JC: 14, 15, 67;
    MJ: 11-13, 36; TP: 166 (see *word*)
  and faith, JC: 44, 100, 101, 175; P: 91, 161
  and praise, (see *praise, whole creation responds to*)
  and time, MG: 44, 45
  as described in Genesis, ASP: 12; CH: 18, 31; JC: 140,
    141; TP: 55
  as evolution of ideas in mind, MG: 45; MJ: 60; P: 4, 5,
    49; TP: 55, 56, 74, 75
  as governed by law and order, KL: 25
  conscious, ASP: 70
  ego-forming capacity of man and, ASP: 19
  Elohim God and, JC: 45
  God as source of all, ASP: 59, 93; KL: 65; MG: 138,
    229, 230; TP: 94; TT: 66, 67, 70
  God is present in all His, JC: 36, 130; MG: 13; TP: 14,
    83, 84

God's conception of, ASP: 99; CH: 18; JC: 16
God vs. man's, CH: 18, 19; KL: 176
health is normal condition of all, JC: 24
Holy Spirit and, ASP: 38, 39
is a cooperation between God and man, CH: 42, 43,
    61-64; JC: 16, 17, 28, 78, 143; TP: 17, 55, 56;
    TT: 70, 71, 92, 93
man as important factor in, ASP: 19, 93-96; CH: 9-11,
    43; KL: 110; TT: 14, 15, 24 (see *man, as co-creator
    with God*)
new, ASP: 95
no evidence of a miraculous, ASP: 139
object of, MG: 45
of man, ASP: 138, 139
of the earth, ASP: 70
science and theological explanation of, ASP: 85
spiritual, MG: 3-5, 9-43, 101
steps in, KL: 19, 61; P: 83-86; CH: 32, 61, 62
trend is upward in all, ASP: 36

creative center, faith-thinking faculty, KL: 114

creative law, (see *law, creative*)

creative Mind, (see *Mind, creative*)

creative source, right conception of, KL: 25

Creator, ASP: 93; CH: 16, 18, 19, 31, 32, 67; JC: 16, 25,
    143, 186; KL: 24, 25, 101; P: 161; TP: 14, 30, 83
    (see *God, as creator*)

creator, ASP: 93, 94

creature(s), MG: 22, 174
  new, MG: 174
  "four living," JC: 151

credit, KL: 51; P: 128

creditors, P: 122, 123, 126, 129

creed, ASP: 54, 78, 79; JC: 91; P: 10; TT: 109, 132, 174
(see *Jesus, and creeds and dogmas*)

creeping things, TP: 56

Crile, Dr. George W., JC: 192

criminals, CH: 124

crisis, TT: 123, 124

criticism, P: 110, 123; TT: 87 (see *condemnation; error*)

crops, P: 139, 140

cross, as a symbol, TM: 70, 156 (see *Jesus, and meaning of the crucifixion; Jesus*)

croup, TT: 17

crown of life, KL: 167

crucifixion, ASP: 42, 144, 155; CH: 59; JC: 163, 184, 185; KL: 194-195; MG: 71; MJ: 145, 154, 161-164, 172, 174; TM: 70; TP: 64; TT: 113, 166 (see *Jesus, crucifixion of*)

Crusades, ASP: 59

crystallization, JC: 97, 172; TM: 145

cults, TP: 124

culture, ASP: 16, 22

cup,
  Jesus', MG: 335
  Joseph's, MG: 335

current, JC: 195; KL: 74
  electrical, JC: 195

D

Damascus, ASP: 26-28; MG: 135, 136

damnation, CH: 123; KL: 98

Dan, MG: 135, 238, 275, 351, 368

Daniel, ASP: 19-21; CH: 103; MG: 188; TM: 81, 94;
TT: 47, 136
(dreams), CH: 102, 103

darkness, MG: 15, 37, 63; MJ: 37, 169; TT: 69

Darwin, Charles Robert, CH: 30; JC: 191, 192; MJ: 36

daughter of God, TM: 53, 55

David, ASP: 100; JC: 77; KL: 31; MG: 41, 221; P: 65,
182, 183, 184, 185; TM: 24, 25, 36; TP: 135, 136

day, MG: 11, 16, 20, 21, 51, 81; P: 83
of judgment (see *judgment, day of*)
seventh, KL: 171; MG: 11, 31

daydreamers, JC: 113, 114

daydreams, CH: 96; MG: 319

dead,
God is not the God of the, ASP: 44
in trespasses and sins, TM: 170
raising the, KL: 98, 99; MJ: 63; TT: 38 (see *Jesus, and
raising of dead*)

deafness, TM: 108
healing of, ASP: 133

deception, TT: 60

Decius, in "Julius Caesar," ASP: 110

decreeing, ASP: 50-55; JC: 178; P: 15, 54; TP: 78, 79, 85, 89

Dedan,
  son of Jokshan, MG: 202, 203
  son of Raamah, MG: 97

dedication, P: 20, 150

deeds, good, ASP: 48

deep, the, MG: 15, 63 (see *sea*)

degeneration, KL: 131; TP: 64

Deity, foundation of, JC: 34; TT: 157

Delilah, TM: 36, 37 (see also *Samson and Delilah*)

delusions, KL: 27, 61, 114

demand and supply, P: 18-19, 53, 73, 93-94

demons, casting out, JC: 89; TM: 66, 142; TT: 158

demonstration of Truth, JC: 120, 133, 134; P: 18, 27, 28, 37, 96
  all, comes through man's mind, P: 32, 56, 177; TP: 39
  and forgiveness, P: 119
  and realization, JC: 39-52
  and Sabbath, MJ: 59
  and thought, JC: 15, 89, 104, 105, 106, 112, 118, 119, 120, 127, 128; MJ: 115, 139; P: 57-86, 92, 93; TP: 74; TT: 29, 116
  as a sign, MJ: 118
  crucifixion as, MJ: 145, 164, 165
  example of, KL: 146

failure to make, reasons for, KL: 18; MJ: 132, 139,
177; P: 13, 67, 84, 97, 111, 112, 118, 119, 147, 157;
TT: 43, 50, 55, 85, 86, 144
Holy Spirit and, MJ: 143
how to make, ASP: 40, 73, 74, 155; CH: 8-11; KL: 18,
64, 106, 120, 170, 171; JC: 109, 133-135; P: 37, 59;
TP: 182, 183
imagination in, JC: 113, 114; P: 100, 101
importance in making one's own, MJ: 100, 143; P: 99
in name of Jesus Christ, ASP: 73-75
is according to one's knowledge of law, P: 58
Jesus and, ASP: 142-149; TT: 166, 167 (see *Jesus;*
Jesus Christ)
love and, MJ: 117; TT: 55, 152, 153
of Christ by thought, ASP: 70-79
of supermind, ASP: 127, 130
of unseen forces, JC: 159
order and, JC: 118, 119
others helped by every, ASP: 42, 43
persistence in, P: 111, 114
prosperity and, P: whole book; TP: 41, 131; TT: 55
through faith, JC: 111; MG: 143, 148, 149; MJ: 74,
75, 111; P: 42, 66, 84, 107; TP: 157-163
through prayer, thanksgiving, and blessing, CH: 78-81,
127; JC: 74, 75, 111; KL: 146; MJ: 67-69;
P: 33-35, 42-55, 57-60, 99, 100; TP: 92 (see *thanks-*
giving, as help in demonstration of supply)
through the word, CH: 68-70; JC: 118, 119, 120;
MJ: 98, 99; TP: 41, 156-163; TT: 130, 131, 154
(see *word*)
why delayed, JC: 15, 19, 61, 117, 122, 123, 125, 175,
176
denial, JC: 47, 61, 131; KL: 70; MG: 360; MJ: 153;
P: 27, 70; TM: 18; TT: 85, 98
and forgiveness of sin, CH: 57, 58; JC: 61, 103
and healing, JC: 1, 37, 129; TP: 131, 154, 155
and soul growth, TP: 67, 96, 99, 154
as agent for disolving appearance of lack, P: 37, 38, 41,
69, 93, 114, 119, 120 121, 122, 123, 151, 157, 170,
177-179
as redeemer of man's consciousness, KL: 195; MJ: 98;

TT: 79
and growth, P: 178; TM: 167
and life, TM: 131
and love, P: 102, 103
and prayer, TP: 4, 127, 128
as forerunner of fulfillment, JC: 47, 192; P: 27, 28
as form of prayer, KL: 146
as moving factor of I AM, TT: 77-83
basically good, TM: 131
denial and affirmation as remedies for sense, TM: 168,
     169
intemperate, MJ: 88, 89
is desire for God, P: 91, 92
is fulfilled through formative word, TM: 150, 151
is inherently good, JC: 100; MG: 280; P: 163
known and answered instantly, JC: 78
of the flesh, P: 160; TM: 146, 147; TT: 40
postulates fulfillment, JC: 133-135; TM: 131; TP: 4
results in sin if manifested erroneously, JC: 60; TP: 128
to excel, KL: 140

destiny, ASP: 52; MG: 65
   of the race, ASP: 52 (see man, destiny of; race, human,
      destiny of)

destructiveness, MG: 289

determination, P: 112

Deuteronomy, KL: 105

devil, ASP: 97; TT: 39, 106 (see Satan)
   as adverse personal will, CH: 115, 116; MJ: 158;
      TM: 66, 69-70; TT: 171
   exists only in sense mind, KL: 61

devotion, TP: 32

diabetes, CH: 54

Diaglott (see Emphatic Diaglott)

diamond, ASP: 49

dictator, TM: 108; TP: 141-143

"die daily," ASP: 43; JC: 163

diet and health, ASP: 51, 52

diffidence, KL: 112

digestion, ASP: 51; P: 174

Diklah, MG: 106

dimension, fourth (see *fourth dimension*)

Dinah, MG: 242, 266, 267, 269, 346, 365, 366

Dinhabah, MG: 289

Diogenes, P: 90, 91, 163; TT: 75

disappointment, CH: 54
  how to relieve, JC: 173

discernment, MG: 274; TP: 154
  spiritual, JC: 92, 93, 103, 139; P: 9, 117; TM: 17, 47,
    67, 84; TP: 71; TT: 111, 164

disciples, ASP: 144-146; JC: 155, 156; MJ: 80, 89,
    142-147; P: 48; TM: 73-77; TP: 16; TT: 38, 101,
    129-132 (see *apostles; Jesus, and His disciples*)
  as egos or identities (see *disciples, as faculties, attributes,
    or powers*)
  as faculties, attributes, or powers, TM: 16, 45, 62, 140;
    TT: 52, 53, 91
  calling of the twelve, CH: 132; TM: 15, 16, 45, 50
  of the Lord, ASP: 26
  spiritual baptism of, ASP: 30, 31
  symbolism of the twelve, CH: 73, 92; MJ: 24, 25, 128,
    134, 135, 169, 170, 177-182; TM: 19, 48, 49, 50, 62,

66 (see *Bhakti; disciples, as faculties, attributes, or power*)

discipline, CH: 114-116, 123, 124, 135; KL: 4; MG: 206, 207; TP: 23, 24
  mental, JC: 97

discomfort, KL: 60

discord, ASP: 148; KL: 59, 65, 68, 175; P: 111; TM: 164; TT: 20, 21, 162
  how to avoid, MJ: 59

discouragement, TM: 66

discovery, ASP: 15, 16, 59, 60, 64, 65

discrimination, ASP: 57, 78; CH: 125, 128; MG: 22, 23, 368; P: 45, 173, 174, 177, 178; TM: 19, 20, 44; TP: 182; TT: 56, 125 (see *James, son of Zebedee*)

discussion, ASP: 74

disease, JC: 132
  and serums, TM: 147, 148
  causes of, ASP: 158; CH: 52-54; JC: 53, 56, 57, 174; KL: 59, 65, 161, 163; P: 96, 148; TM: 22, 23, 57-59, 134, 145-147, 165-169; TP: 178, 179; TT: 17-26
  germs, ASP: 104; JC: 173, 174; TT: 17-26
  how healed, ASP: 46; CH: 69, 70; JC: 56-66; P: 148; TM: 120; TP: 58, 59, 130, 131, 178, 179; TT: 115, 116
  no incurable, ASP: 132
  not natural, KL: 22; MJ: 109; TP: 130, 131; TT: 120
  not of God, TT: 56
  thinking body into, CH: 45, 47, 54, 64-66, 69, 105 (see *thought, as source of disease*)
  vs. health, ASP: 71, 72; TT: 39

Dishan, MG: 284, 288

Dishon, MG: 284, 286

disobedience, JC: 53; TM: 108; TT: 96

dissipation, P: 160

distribution, P: 128, 135

distrust, P: 118

divine law (see *law, divine*)

Divine Mind (see *Mind, Divine*)

divine Mother, TP: 31

Divinity, MJ: 141

divinity, MJ: 38, 39 (see *Jesus, divinity of*)

Dodanim, MG: 95

doctor of medicine, P: 154

doctors, JC: 80, 104, 107, 109, 132, 168, 182; TM: 134, 148; TT: 120

doctrine, KL: 32, 33, (see *Jesus Christ, original doctrine of*)

dogma, TM: 111, 112; TT: 104, 105, 132, 133, 138, 139

dominion, ASP: 34, 53, 63; MG: 185, 274; P: 92, 124; TT: 142 (see *mastery; power*)
  affirmation for, KL: 154, 181; TP: 182
  exercised by man, ASP: 63, 66, 68; CH: 32, 36, 47, 48, 51, 115, 116; JC: 22, 43, 186; KL: 67, 68, 153, 180; MG: 25, 47-48; MJ: 12, 32, 103, 104; P: 80, 92, 96, 97, 155, 156, 160, 161, 182-184; TM: 44, 61-70, 113, 120, 140, 169; TT: 25, 89, 90, 93, 109
  over spiritual ideas, ASP: 34, 68, 82

spiritual, ASP: 30, 45-47, 53, 63

door, MJ: 100, 102; P: 32
  into the kingdom of God, ASP: 136

Dothan, MG: 297, 298

Double-mindedness, CH: 9, 125; KL: 44, 87, 88, 92;
    MG: 98, 123, 129, 303, 304, 306, 321, 322, 349;
    P: 59; TM: 89, 90; TP: 101, 124, 130, 158, 160,
    172, 173; TT: 10, 45, 147

doubt, CH: 88, 116, 117; JC: 68, 106, 148, 149;
    MG: 153; P: 44
  impedes manifestation, P: 44, 46, 47; KL: 18, 20;
    MG: 30
  vs. confidence, ASP: 74, 75
  vs. faith in expression of Truth, P: 45, 85, 123, 172

dove, MG: 83, 93

dread, TP: 179

dreamers, CH: 102; JC: 113, 114; MJ: 22

dreams, JC: 82, 195, 196; TT: 150 (see *visions; imagi-
    nation*)
  Abimelich's, MG: 173
  Abraham's, MG: 144, 145 (see *Abraham, vision of*)
  and genius, JC: 113
  and spiritual experiences, CH: 36, 101-104
  and superconscious mind, P: 31, 32
  and vital forces, ASP: 158
  as means of communication between God and man,
    CH: 102, 103; MG: 139, 219, 220; TP: 51, 144,
    145; TT: 136
  Daniel's interpretation of, ASP: 19, 20, 110, 111;
    TT: 136, 137
  God and, ASP: 20
  I AM and subconscious mind in, ASP: 109
  imagination and, MG: 295; KL: 155

E

Eadie's "Bible Cyclopedia," CH: 18

ears, ASP: 56, 57; TM: 108, 140, 141; TP: 116-118, 154
   affirmation for improving, TM: 141; TP: 154
   and excessive meditation, TP: 117, 118
   as auditory center in brain, TP: 117
   healing of, ASP: 133

earth, ASP: 50, 51, 52, 68, 70; JC: 187; KL: 41, 184;
      P: 90, 91, 104, 167; TM: 149, 150
   consciousness (see *consciousness, earth*)
   creation of the, MG: 3, 4, 12, 18-28
   earthquakes, ASP: 29; TM: 148, 149
   heaven and, ASP: 21, 43; JC: 74, 187; MG: 3, 4, 12,
      163, 164; P: 176, 177; TM: 17, 18, 28, 29, 68, 69;
      TP: 48
   new, ASP: 16, 21, 39, 51, 53, 54, 162, 163; CH: 138,
      139; TM: 69; TT: 125

east, MG: 34, 48, 93, 233; TP: 49

Easter, ASP: 143; KL: 3, 139, 197

eating, TM: 136, 157 (see *diet*)
   and health, CH: 41; TP: 79; TT: 153, 154
   and thinking, ASP: 72, 73
   appetite and, TP: 105
   as symbol of mental appropriation, P: 71; TT: 146
   Jesus on, JC: 81, 177, 178
   of body of Jesus, KL: 192; TM: 120; TP: 65, 68, 69
   of bread, MG: 158, 253
   of fruit of the tree of knowledge, CH: 47, 56; MG: 34,
      38, 39, 49, 50, 68; MJ: 36; TM: 57, 58, 104, 168
   of meat, MG: 85
   Paul on, ASP: 20, 21 (see *diet*)
   words of Truth, KL: 12

Ebal, MG: 285

Eber, MG: 103, 105

economic,
  conditions, ASP: 31, 32
  problems, TP: 98, 99, 128 (see *problems, world*)
  panacea for healing of, TP: 98, 99

economics, P: 147 (see *Jesus, economic system inaugurated by disciples of; religion, economics and*)

economy, P: 115, 152, 167, 168, 170, 186
  new, ASP: 34, 35

Eden (see *Garden of Eden*)
  as allegory, JC: 177, 178; KL: 130
  as state of mind, KL: 115; MG: 124; MJ: 62, 63; TM: 56, 169; TT: 45, 137, 147, 161
  man's body as, KL: 147; TM: 163

Eder (tower), MG: 274

Edison, Thomas Alva, ASP: 64; JC: 45; KL: 69

editors, JC: 119, 120

Edmond, in "King Lear," ASP: 113

Edom (or Esau), MG: 210, 211, 279, 290, 292 (see *Esau*)
  land of, MG: 257, 289, 290

Edomites, MG: 283

education, moral and spiritual, ASP: 53, 54, 60, 88-91; JC: 33 (see *mind, education of*)

effect, TP: 34 (see *thought, and effect*)

efficiency, P: 111, 141, 142

effort, P: 33, 63, 64

ego, ASP: 19, 30; CH: 46, 50; KL: 55; MG: 318, 357;
    P: 44; TM: 5, 6, 150, 161, 162, 164, 165; TT: 36,
    81, 158, 162, 165
  as I AM, CH: 121; KL: 121; JC: 14; P: 118; TT: 36,
    68, 77, 78, 157
  life, TM: 161
  personal, CH: 58, 59, 64, 131; MG: 109, 137, 184, 200;
    TM: 66, 69, 70
  spiritual, ASP: 43, 123; CH: 59, 131; KL: 119;
    MG: 137, 374; TM: 130; TT: 159

egotism, KL: 112; MG: 144, 170; MJ: 87; TM: 162;
    TP: 113
  as destroying spirituality, ASP: 103; MG: 120;
    TP: 150-152
  repression of, ASP: 102, 103

Egypt, ASP: 161; CH: 102; JC: 164; KL: 56; MG: 144,
    152, 295, 301, 320, 352, 370, 373, 374; TM: 98,
    102, 103, 120, 121, 124, 126
  and substance, MG: 329, 352
  as materialism, ASP: 54
  as seat of body consciousness, MG: 120-124, 134, 307,
    308, 323-325, 327, 330, 332, 339-342, 354, 355, 375
  as subconscious realm, MG: 145, 321, 335

Egyptians, JC: 55; MG: 334, 339, 342, 373; TM: 121;
    TT: 17

Ehi, or Aharah, MG: 350

Einstein, Albert (quoted), JC: 49, 50; TM: 86-88

El, JC: 141; MG: 193

Elah, MG: 292

Elam,
  country of, MG: 129

son of Shem, MG: 103

El-beth-el (holy place), MG: 271

Eldaah, MG: 203

electricity, JC: 147, 194, 195; P: 12, 102; TT: 41, 42,
  130, 148
  and atomic energy, ASP: 12-17; JC: 20, 42-45;
    MJ: 174, 181; P: 10
  and faith, ASP: 12, 14, 15, 125, 126; JC: 44, 45
  and matter, JC: 142
  as form of radiant substance, TP: 39
  laws of mind vs. laws of, KL: 47-48
  modern scientific view on, KL: 132

electrons, ASP: 13, 14, 84, 125; CH: 44; JC: 145, 149,
  174; P: 75; TP: 65, 109
  spiritual, KL: 26, 164, 166; TM: 4, 5

El-Elohe-Israel, MG: 265

elements,
  and mind, ASP: 29
  chemical, JC: 42
  control of, TM: 31, 108 (see *Elijah, and control of
    elements*)

eleven, TM: 98

Eliezer (of Damascus), MG: 144

Elijah, ASP: 9, 10, 127, 156; CH: 80, 127; JC: 75, 126;
  KL: 3, 69; P: 33-34, 134; TM: 89; TP: 72, 137;
  TT: 9, 58
  and control of elements, ASP: 127; CH: 80; JC: 75;
    P: 33, 34, 134; TP: 72
  as example of penitence, KL: 138 (fulfillment),
    ASP: 156, 157
  penetrated atoms by power of thought, ASP: 9, 10;
    KL: 179

elimination, MG: 275; P: 98, 99, 178, 179; TM: 21, 158
   (see *renunciation*)

Eliphaz, JC: 144; MG: 277, 279, 280; TP: 85

Elisabeth, P: 44

Elisha, ASP: 9, 125; JC: 75
  and Naaman the Syrian, TP: 148-154
  and law of prosperity, P: 99-101, 113-114; TP: 33, 34
  and widow, ASP: 125; TP: 34

Elishah, MG: 95

Ellasar, MG: 129

Elohim, CH: 32; JC: 141; MG: 28; TM: 53, 54

Elohim God, JC: 45, 141, 158, 186; KL: 132, 177;
   MG: 15, 28, 29, 32-34, 78, 192, 193; TP: 55;
   TT: 14

Elon,
  son of Zebulun, MG: 346
  the Hittite, MG: 217, 218

El-paran (region), MG: 132, 133

El Shaddai ("Almighty," "Nourisher," or "Strength-giver"),
   ASP: 98; MG: 150; MJ: 73, 74

emergency, ASP: 52

Emerson (quoted), ASP: 34, 137, 138; JC: 87, 149, 174;
   P: 112; TM: 9, 138-139, 169; TP: 36, 57, 58;
   P: 112; TT: 9, 26

Emim (race of giants), MG: 132

Emmaus, ASP: 145, 146

emotion, CH: 101, 110; JC: 27, 33; MG: 36, 55, 165, 166, 237, 281; TM: 20, 64, 69, 133, 134; TP: 91, 107, 114, 132-134; TT: 152, 153, 158

Emphatic Diaglott (quoted), ASP: 162, 170

empty vessels, P: 113

Enaim, or Enam (city), MG: 306

end,
  in Spirit there is no, KL: 46
  of the age (world), KL: 26, 27, 40, 41; JC: 20

enemy, TT: 87, 112

energy, JC: 42, 43, 138, 145, 168; P: 159, 160, 176; TM: 135, 136, 158; TP: 23, 61, 79, 89, 109, 126; TT: 43
  and cells of body, ASP: 13, 14, 41; KL: 132; TM: 5; TP: 60, 61, 79
  and matter, JC: 145, 146, 149
  and prayer, ASP: 40; JC: 76; TM: 5, 123
  and thought, ASP: 14; JC: 19, 39, 43, 94, 105, 138
  and words, JC: 90, 137, 174; KL: 166; TP: 34, 91, 92
  as life source, KL: 125, 132 (see *life, as energy*)
  atomic, ASP: 13-17, 50, 51, 52, 60, 65; MG: 368; P: 48 (see *electricity, and atomic energy*)
  divine, JC: 24; TP: 18
  dynamic, ASP: 66
  electronic, ASP: 14, 15, 41; P: 10; TM: 5, 6
  etheric, ASP: 10, P: 10, 12; TP: 97
  Holy Spirit as dynamic, ASP: 66, 67
  in man's body, ASP: 11, 41, 101; JC: 76, 145, 146; MG: 320, 321; MJ: 27, 181; TM: 4, 5, 6, 63; TP: 68
  is never lost, ASP: 51
  is zeal in motion, TM: 130, 136
  Jesus and, JC: 145, 146
  man may use to construct or to destroy, ASP: 53
  mental, JC: 43; TM: 4; P: 13; TP: 80, 81, 142
  primal, JC: 172

Er, MG: 303, 345

era, new, ASP: 21, 22, 34, 35, 165; P: 9, 23, 80, 126-128, 145, 149-151, 164, 172

Erech, MG: 98

Eri, MG: 347

error, CH: 123; KL: 59, 60, 141; TM: 45
  consciousness (see *consciousness, error*)
  has no power in itself, KL: 141
  ideas, P: 180, 181
  is not of God, TM: 42, 43; TP: 129-131; TT: 24, 25, 162, 163
  may be deeply rooted in subconscious, KL: 127, 193
  negative talk is, P: 46; TT: 87, 116, 117
  overcoming of, ASP: 38, 49; CH: 57, 58; JC: 59, 60, 62, 63, 129, 151, 193; KL: 12, 98, 99; MG: 168, 258, 300; P: 175, 180; TT: 107, 108 (see *mind, dissolving error states in*)
    by denial, KL: 64, 65, 141; TM: 21, 152, 153
    by outworking of divine law, MG: 133, 217, 299
    by working of Spirit in the subconscious, ASP: 76; CH: 108, 109
    Jesus' three days in tomb symbolize three steps in, KL: 195
    joy in, KL: 189
  spiritual fire is symbol of destruction of, KL: 191
  thought (see *thought, error*)
  why encountered following exaltation, ASP: 155

Esau, MG: 221, 252, 283, 292
  as body consciousness, MG: 209-212, 217, 218, 220, 221, 223, 227, 232, 252, 254, 257-259, 261-263, 276-285, 292
  as entitled to blessing of firstborn, KL: 78-82; TP: 139, 140
  is supplanted by Jacob, KL: 78-82; MG: 220-225, 232, 254, 257-259; TP: 139-147
  represents natural man, or body, CH: 101; KL: 79-82;

MG: 210, 211, 212, 254, 257-259, 261-263, 276, 277, 278, 279; TP: 139-147

Esdras, TM: 63

Esek (well), MG: 215

Eshban, MJ: 286, 287

Eshcol, MG: 135

eternal life (see *life, eternal*)

eternity, JC: 121

ether, ASP: 54; CH: 62, 63, 68, 99, 100, 103, 104;
    MG: 34, 35, 368; MJ: 69, 70, 174, 175; TT: 163
  all life originates in, JC: 140
  and omnipresent Mind, JC: 140
  and space, JC: 143; KL: 132
  and supply, ASP: 10; P: 55, 90, 91; TT: 55, 61
  and the spoken word, ASP: 54, 55; TP: 19, 74, 77
  and thought, CH: 63, 68
  cosmic, MG: 34, 38, 368
  and Christ mind, JC: 150
  as "kingdom of the heavens," ASP: 10, 11, 40, 58, 169;
    P: 12, 54; TM: 8, 9
  faith and spiritual, ASP: 125
  hearing capacity extended into spiritual, ASP: 56, 57
  in science and metaphysics, P: 10-12, 54, 80; TP: 15,
    43, 71, 97, 109, 110, 131
  nature of, MJ: 169; TM: 29; TP: 52, 53
  signs of "second coming" in, ASP: 169, 170
  spiritual, JC: 78, 83, 84, 157; KL: 11; TP: 19, 29, 32,
    74, 75, 139

eugenics, ASP: 33, 34

Euphrates (river), MG: 38, 146

Europe, ASP: 51, 52, 59; P: 127

Eutychus, TP: 162

Eve, CH: 31, 112; JC: 178; KL: 130; MG: 41, 42, 55, 56, 65; MJ: 24; P: 72; TM: 35, 37, 40, 41, 43, 57, 169; TP: 52, 64

evening, MG: 17, 21

events, MG: 44

evil, ASP: 114, 155, 172; KL: 127; TM: 155; TT: 39, 125
    denial as aid to, KL: 152; TP: 105; TT: 22, 39, 40, 56, 57
    dissolution of consciousness of, KL: 152; MG: 35, 36, 39, 43, 45, 46, 48, 57, 68, 123, 129, 265, 350, 351; TM: 57, 58, 59, 150; TP: 105; TT: 56, 117, 150
    duality of consciousness and, CH: 56; KL: 60, 87, 88, 114, 115; MG: 35, 36, 39, 43, 68, 98, 123, 129, 350, 351; MJ: 36, 37, 59, 60; TM: 41-45, 57, 58, 59, 104; TP: 172, 173; TT: 22
    fear of, MG: 350, 351; TP: 105, 113
    how to become impregnable to, MJ: 150, 151
    Jesus and, JC: 57; MJ: 5
    love and, MG: 299; TT: 56, 60
    no power in, CH: 57, 58
    on pronouncing nothing, CH: 93
    sensation and, MG: 35, 36, 47-50, 57
    spirits, TT: 158
    sublimation of, MG: 291
    Truth statements for healing of, TP: 96, 105, 114, 175

evolution, MG: 59 (see *consciousness, evolution of; man, evolution of*)
    economic, ASP: 34, 35, 61; JC: 150; KL: 82; P: 147
    involution precedes, MG: 14, 25, 26, 323; TM: 121
    Jesus and, JC: 54, 55 (see *Jesus, evolution of*)
    law of, KL: 158; MJ: 33, 36, 37, 97, 98; TM: 38
    Lot represents faith in a state of, MG: 169
    moves in cycles, MG: 171; TT: 16
    of consciousness (see *consciousness, evolution of*)

F

face, ASP: 83, 157
  horned, ASP: 83
  illumined, ASP: 83, 84
  of ground, MG: 33

faculties of man, twelve, CH: 85-93, 107-117, 119-129, 130-141; MG: 20; MJ: 32; P: 18, 19, 64, 79, 161; TP: 15, 127 (see *powers; man, faculties or powers of; mind, faculties of*)
  are evolved on three planes, JC: 71; MG: 238, 239, 325
  are used by I AM, MJ: 68
  mental aspects of, CH: 96; KL: 80, 110, 112, 113, 116, 117, 119, 147; TM: 16, 21, 23, 28, 39, 40, 44, 45, 46, 50, 62, 71, 83, 91, 97, 98, 104, 131, 132
  misuse of, MG: 75, 274, 324, 351; TT: 58
  represented by,
    disciples of Jesus, MG: 11, 12, 232, 243; MJ: 20, 32, 84, 170
    sons of Jacob, CH: 72; MG: 11, 232, 242, 243, 293, 323-352; P: 45; TT: 90, 91
  spiritual aspects of, CH: 72-81, 85-93, 101, 102, 107-117, 119-129, 130-141; JC: 72, 152, 173; MG: 73, 74, 177, 178, 231, 232, 236, 237, 239, 242, 243, 247, 254, 274, 310, 311, 323, 329, 330, 341, 342, 353-376
  wither away if not used, MJ: 137

failure, ASP: 75, 76, 105; CH: 54, 80; KL: 45, 59, 60; P: 69; TP: 40, 46, 82, 111

faith, ASP: 10, 11, 30, 104, 125-133; CH: 80, 81, 85-95; JC: 15, 44, 53, 61, 74, 100-116, 144, 156, 195; KL: 38, 110-121, 133, 148 (see *Benjamin; Peter; pineal gland; prayer*)
  Abraham as representing (see *Abraham*)
  affirmations for development of, CH: 94, 95; KL: 149

and All-Presence, CH: 66, 67
and blessing, ASP: 102
and creation, JC: 44, 100, 101, 175; P: 91, 161
and debts, P: 126
and demonstration (see *demonstration, through faith*)
and giving, P: 134
and healing, ASP: 11, 76, 101, 126, 131; CH: 66, 67;
    JC: 53, 56, 74, 75, 76, 101, 103, 105, 156; KL: 4,
    28, 173, 174; MJ: 54, 55; TP: 27-32, 152, 153, 155,
    164, 165, 178; TT: 49
and ideas, CH: 90; JC: 35, 101, 114, 175; KL: 119;
    P: 43, 78, 79, 91, 161, 170; TM: 28, 29; TP: 32
and life, MG: 181; MJ: 41, 110, 111; TP: 149, 150
and love, ASP: 40; JC: 103; KL: 119, 120; MG: 126;
    MJ: 128, 179, 180
and manifestation, MJ: 132, 133; P: 42-55, 64, 65;
    TP: 31
and material remedies, JC: 104, 107
and matter, ASP: 40
and perception, P: 43, 44
and prayer, ASP: 11; CH: 76, 77, 88, 89; JC: 72, 74,
    79; TP: 28, 39, 32, 157-163
and spoken word, ASP: 55; TM: 29-30, 39, 45;
    TP: 27-32, 77
and subconscious, MG: 17, 116; P: 45
and substance, CH: 86, 87; MG: 331, 332; MJ: 20, 74,
    75, 177; P: 42-55; TP: 28, 39, 68, 69
and supply, MJ: 180, 181; P: 17, 18, 42-55, 138 (see
    supply, faith and)
and understanding, CH: 37; JC: 72; MJ: 81; P: 45, 84
as basically spiritual, JC: 101, 102
as basis of all action, JC: 101, 107; KL: 148
as essential to success, CH: 85-91 (see *success*)
as ever active, CH: 90
as factor in practical life, P: 50, 54
as faculty of mind, CH: 85-93; KL: 110-121, 147, 148;
    MG: 195
as foundation of consciousness, KL: 114, 115, 117
as foundation of prosperity, ASP: 125; CH: 136; P: 13,
    20, 42-55, 66, 74, 75, 84, 134, 135, 144, 170
as foundation or firmament, MG: 16, 17, 19, 20, 31, 32

Jesus Christ and (see *Jesus Christ, and faith*)
  miraculous power of, JC: 75, 101; KL: 117
  negative, MG: 73, 74, 119, 123, 134, 165, 167
  not limited to religious experience, CH: 85, 86
  Paul on, CH: 85; JC: 74, 75; MG: 116
  Peter as representing (see *Peter*)
  pineal gland as center of (see *pineal gland*)
  power and, MJ: 70, 71
  prayer of, JC: 70; TP: 29
  productive results of active, MG: 142, 143
  quickens spiritual forces in man, ASP: 126; CH: 135;
    JC: 10, 11, 15, 44, 45, 74, 75, 135, 156, 166, 167,
    175, 176; KL: 21, 133
  relation of to mind, MG: 17, 116
  Reuben as representing (see *Reuben*)
  seat of, TM: 16, 17, 31
  thought and, ASP: 74; KL: 110-121; TT: 90
  tithing and, P: 134, 138
  vs. doubt, JC: 106
  wisdom and, ASP: 75; P: 124, 125

faithfulness, ASP: 39; MG: 311; TP: 35

Faith-thinking, KL: 110
  food of, KL: 119
  most important power of man, KL: 113
  nature of, KL: 119

fall,
  of man (see *man, fall of*)
  of Satan from heaven, TM: 162

falling, dream of, ASP: 158

fame, P: 161

family, CH: 131, 132, 135; KL: 53; TT: 80, 81

famine, KL: 133; MG: 120, 325, 329, 330, 357; P: 20,
    46, 63, 85, 90, 97, 134

fanaticism, MJ: 119

"far country," P: 62, 63

farmer, P: 104, 105, 137, 139, 140, 170

farming, P: 105
  and tithing, P: 138-140

Farrar, Archdeacon (quoted), CH: 123, 124

fasting, KL: 3, 4, 5, 6, 138, 140; MJ: 51, 75; TT: 171
  (see *Jesus, and fasting*)

fate, ASP: 15

Father, ASP: 157; P: 35, 36, 82; TT: 74, 90-92, 105,
    133, 134, 141, 144, 159, 174
  access to, through Jesus Christ, ASP: 62; JC: 19, 84;
    TP: 65; TT: 141, 142, 166
  and forgiveness, P: 118-119, 122
  and Son (see *Son, Father and*)
  as all-providing substance, P: 38, 39, 40, 51, 56, 57,
    61-63, 68, 75, 81, 98, 122, 144, 186
  as Christ, CH: 67
  as God-Mind, KL: 173; MJ: 137
  asking in name of Jesus Christ, TP: 84, 85
  as man's protector, TT: 94, 95, 108
  as omnipresent intelligence, CH: 11; MJ: 86, 146;
    TT: 72
  as part of Trinity, CH: 20; KL: 14-18; MJ: 92, 93;
    TT: 134
  as principle of life within man, CH: 122; JC: 16;
    MJ: 61, 130, 131
  as principle, MJ: 136
  as provider, JC: 18, 68, 109; KL: 107; MJ: 178, 180;
    P: 61, 62, 68, 74, 75, 90; TP: 85
  as source of power and wisdom, TT: 38
  as Spirit, JC: 98, 99; TM: 122
  as supermind, TP: 5, 81, 82
  communion with, ASP: 21, 94, 95; TM: 115, 116, 117

connection of man's indwelling life with, MJ: 168, 180
defined, TP: 5
finding the, in man's inner temple, TM: 116; TT: 33, 34, 35, 97, 98
glory of, made manifest through Son, TT: 24
God as, CH: 15, 16; MJ: 60, 90; TT: 178
going direct to, MJ: 146
"I and the, are one," ASP: 37; TP: 13
indwelling, JC: 187, 190; KL: 87, 88, 89; MJ: 61, 62, 74, 75, 92, 93, 105, 146, 174; P: 62, 63, 68, 74, 75; TM: 54, 115; TP: 3; TT: 35-37, 42 (see *Jesus, and indwelling Father*)
Jehovah as, ASP: 10; JC: 141; TM: 54, 106
Jesus on man's unity with, CH: 25
Jesus' recognition of mind as, ASP: 40
Jesus' unity with, JC: 141; MJ: 129, 131, 132, 133, 149; TP: 17, 87; TT: 142, 166, 172, 173
judgment and the, CH: 122
Logos as, TP: 168-174
man's oneness with, ASP: 29, 68, 69, 71, 104; JC: 143; KL: 13; MJ: 16, 131, 132, 149; TP: 84; TT: 98, 99, 142, 143, 166

"father of lights," TP: 120, 121

fathers of the Greek church, TP: 166, 167

father, P: 61, 62, 102, 186

Father's house (see *house, Father's*)

Father-Mind (see *Mind, Father-*)

Father-Mother, P: 36

Father-Mother God, TP: 40, 41

"fatted calf," P: 62

fear, ASP: 103; P: 172; TP: 52, 53 (see *mind, fear and*)
as a habit, TP: 112, 113

as a breeder of poverty, P: 52, 53, 81, 103, 109, 156, 165, 166, 185

as cause of stagnation in circulation of money, KL: 105, 106; P: 47-48, 103, 156; TP: 47, 112

cause of, MG: 100, 132, 138, 257, 259; P: 124, 181; TT: 19

effects of, ASP: 104, 157; CH: 114; JC: 53, 168, 169, 177; MG: 97; MJ: 63; P: 81, 109, 152, 156, 182; TP: 112, 113; TT: 21, 45, 53

love and (see *love, and fear*)
   of evil, MG: 350, 351; TP: 105, 113
   of God, TP: 113

man's relation to, ASP: 27, 28, 62, 78, 96; CH: 16, 26; JC: 50, 67, 74, 135; KL: 51, 55, 88, 124, 168-174, 178; MJ: 131-134

Mind as, MJ: 73; TP: 81, 82

of lack—treatment for overcoming, P: 92, 118, 142, 156, 182, 183, 186 (see *lack, fear of, and how to overcome it*)

of power of money, KL: 105; P: 181, 182

Son, and Holy Ghost, CH: 20; JC: 64, 121, 122; KL: 14-18; MJ: 92, 93; TT: 68, 134

Truth statements for healing, JC: 153; P: 92, 118, 142, 156, 182, 183, 185, 186; TP: 105, 112, 179

vs. love, TP: 112-115; MG: 281

"worketh even until now," ASP: 18; CH: 43; MJ: 60; P: 86

feast, MG: 160; MJ: 28, 56, 114; P: 20, 46, 62

feasting, KL: 5, 6

feeling, CH: 73, 115; JC: 27, 33; MG: 57, 365; TM: 43, 46, 47; TP: 155; TT: 10, 20, 84, 158 (see *emotion*)

feet, ASP: 19, 22; MJ: 126, 127; P: 61; TM: 59
  anointing, of Jesus, MJ: 115, 116
  washing of, MG: 158

fellowship, KL: 35; TP: 14
  with God, JC: 25; MG: 277

feminine, MG: 185, 200, 266, 277, 303, 391; TM: 57, 59
  (see *principle, feminine*)

Fenton, Ferrar, MG: 3, 15, 21, 109; MJ: 12
  on Lord's Prayer, TP: 3; KL: 108

fever, ASP: 148; JC: 56; KL: 64, 65

"fields white already unto harvest," ASP: 32

fig, MG: 51

finances, ASP: 105; KL: 84, 85, 86, 101, 102, 103, 104,
    105; P: 20, 30, 124, 179; TP: 146
  and selfishness, P: 127, 128, 138, 139, 148, 149

financier, KL: 84

fire, TP: 121
  flame of, TM: 7, 123, 124
  of God, KL: 191
  of Spirit, TM: 6, 128; TP: 32
  symbolism of, MG: 94
  tongues of, KL: 53, 191
  zeal is inward, ASP: 26

firmament, MG: 17, 19-20, 140; P: 83

first born, MG: 349; TM: 127 (see *blessing, of firstborn
    child*)

first cause, TT: 134

first fruit, ASP: 130, 131

fisherman, KL: 116

fishes, JC: 145; KL: 119; MG: 23; MJ: 177, 178; P: 91
  (see *loaves and fishes*)

five thousand, ASP: 10

flame invisible, ASP: 24 (see *sword, flame of*)

flesh, KL: 19; TM: 69, 146
   and Spirit—Jesus on, TT: 75, 76
   as food, ASP: 20, 21; MG: 85; TM: 78
   as man's obedient servant, TT: 79
   as state of consciousness, TT: 77-88
   consciousness (see *consciousness, flesh*)
   Esau as representing, KL: 79, 80; TP: 143
   eternal life in the, ASP: 121-124; TT: 77-88
   Jesus Christ incarnated into the, ASP: 24
   man, KL: 58, 81, 82
   mind of the, ASP: 121; KL: 131, 132
   not to be condemned, TT: 79
   saving, from corruption, KL: 20, 21, 151
   symbols of, KL: 81
   vs. spirit, MJ: 112, 126, 127; TT: 75-88

"flesh and blood," CH: 34

flesh-eating, ASP: 20, 21, 51; MG: 85; TM: 78 (see *meat*)

flock, MG: 354

Flood, MG: 72, 74-84, 87, 90

flood, MG: 71, 72, 74, 84, 90; P: 137

floor, threshing, MG: 373, 374

flowers, CH: 65, 66

food, ASP: 16, 51, 52; JC: 120; MG: 35, 85; MJ: 51, 74,
    75; P: 32, 33, 80, 81, 104, 105, 174, 187; TP: 30,
    80, 105; TT: 153, 154 (see *appetite*)
   blessing one's, ASP: 72, 73, 77; MJ: 68; P: 24, 84
   effect of, on receptivity to Spirit, ASP: 20, 21
   meat as (see *flesh; flesh-eating; meat*)

forces, MG: 291; TP: 110; TT: 58, 59
   behind a decree, ASP: 50, 54, 55

body cells as centers of (see *cells, body, as centers of force*)
dynamic, P: 10
invisible, omnipresent, ASP: 18
magnetic, CH: 40, 41
spiritual, ASP: 160, 161
unseen, JC: 159, 160
utilizing and controlling atomic, ASP: 12, 13, 65, 66
vital, ASP: 158

forehead, JC: 152; MJ: 44, 171; P: 183; TP: 25; CH: 109

forgiveness, JC: 61, 68; MG: 337; TT: 87
affirmation for, KL: 169
and healing, JC: 5, 57, 58, 60, 61
and peace, P: 119
and thought, JC: 60, 61
and understanding, JC: 60, 61
Jesus on, P: 109, 117
of others, JC: 58, 59, 68
of sin, CH: 57; JC: 5, 58-61, 68; KL: 35, 160; MJ: 17; P: 119; TP: 152, 173, 174, 175
significance of, JC: 58, 59

form, ASP: 19, 97, 134; JC: 29, 31, 35, 36, 41, 44, 45, 50, 51; TM: 71, 72, 98; TT: 70, 71

formative, TM: 29

formed, the, CH: 19, 32, 34, 36, 38, 50, 62, 64, 99, 103; KL: 14, 15; MG: 39, 45; MJ: 36, 68; P: 14, 15, 56, 75, 76, 78, 79, 91, 94, 95, 100 (see *unformed; earth; imagination*)

formless, the, CH: 32, 36, 38, 64; JC: 78, 79; KL: 14; MG: 39, 45, 349; MJ: 36; P: 14, 43, 56, 75, 76, 78, 79, 95; TT: 70, 71

formula (see *Jesus, formulas of*)

fortune, worldly, KL: 44, 45

forty, KL: 3

fountainhead of life, JC: 80, 98

fountain, of pure life, KL: 123; MG: 149

fourth dimension, ASP: 56-62; KL: 170, 171; TM: 5, 8,
  144, 156
  thinking in the, ASP: 56, 62; MJ: 23; TP: 68 (see
    kingdom of heaven)

fowls, MG: 23

Fox, George, journal of, TM: 80

Fox sisters, ASP: 111

Franklin, Benjamin, TP: 81

freedom, CH: 112; KL: 66, 113; MG: 107; MJ: 88-89,
    112; P: 170; TT: 7, 104 (see *mind, freedom of, and
    search for truth; Spirit, frees man*)
  and personal will, CH: 113-116; KL: 181
  as gift to man from God, ASP: 19, 52, 53; CH: 108,
    109, 112, 113; JC: 23; KL: 156; MJ: 90; TM: 101,
    102, 116, 145; TP: 101
  from bondage to letter of law, ASP: 78
  from debt through prayer, P: 126, 129
  from material limitations, CH: 27
  from worry, JC: 142; P: 110, 122, 142; TM: 128
  of thought, TT: 104
  ways to demonstrate, KL: 64, 65, 66; P: 124-130;
    TM: 67, 127, 128
  through forgiveness, JC: 60, 61
  through Jesus Christ, ASP: 82, 167; JC: 165; KL: 93;
    MJ: 33, 89, 140; TM: 67; TP: 22, 23
  Truth statements for attaining, CH: 114, 116; JC: 37,
    38; P: 130; TP: 183-188

free will, ASP: 19, 53, 78, 118, 119; JC: 177; KL: 29, 55,
    119; TM: 103, 104, 131-132; TP: 124 (see *will, free*)
  and creation, ASP: 96, 97

free will offerings, P: 149, 150, 153, 155

friend, P: 109-110

friendship, MG: 113, 127

Froebel, Friedrich, TM: 39

front brain, (see *brain, front*)

frost, P: 137

fruit, MJ: 137, 138 (see *tree of knowledge*)
  of the Spirit, ASP: 79

fruitfulness, MG: 141, 142, 146

fugitive, MG: 148

fulfillment, MJ: 111 (see *Spirit*)
  affirmation for, TP: 132
  and faith, ASP: 74, 75; MG: 142-144
  functions, physical, MG: 162, 163, 177

  of law (see *law, fulfillment of*)
  represented by Elijah, ASP: 156, 157
  spiritual, JC: 131; MJ: 111, 139; TP: 60-65

future, ASP: 157; KL: 45, 46, (see *prophecy*)
  laying up for, P: 152

G

Gabbatha, MJ: 161

Gad, MG: 239, 275, 276, 351, 368 (see *power, Gad as representing*)

Gaham, MG: 187

Galeed, MG: 252 (see *Jegar-sahadutha*)

Galilee, KL: 75; MJ: 24-26, 46, 47, 52, 77, 169, 170; P: 48

Galli-Curci, Amelita, TM: 65

Galton, Sir Francis (quoted), ASP: 33, 34

ganglion, CH: 75

ganglionic centers, MG: 321 (see *centers, ganglionic*)

garden, MJ: 152; TP: 95

Garden of Eden, JC: 158; KL: 74; MJ: 61; TP: 95, 124; TT: 15, 96 (see *Eden*)
  as allegory, CH: 31, 34, 37, 38, 47, 48, 55, 56; JC: 177, 178; KL: 130; MG: 24, 25, 38, 45; TP: 97; TT: 36, 151
  as antedating formation of earth, TT: 163
  as divine consciousness, CH: 37; MG: 50, 57, 58
  as etheric universe, MG: 34, 35, 38
  as kingdom of the heavens, P: 54, 96, 97
  gates of, as representing faculties of mind, KL: 147
  in man, CH: 47, 48, 70; MG: 34, 35, 38, 39
  man's body as outer expression of, KL: 147; MG: 52; TM: 163, 167, 168
  restoration of, on earth, TT: 122, 123

to dress, MG: 38

garment, MG: 294, 295; MJ: 162; P: 24, 78, 79

Gatam, MG: 279

gate, TT: 96

"gates," as faculties of mind, KL: 147

Gaza, Philistine city, MG: 102; TM: 18, 19

Gehenna, CH: 123, 124; TM: 5, 6 (see *Hinnom, Valley of*)

generation, ASP: 31, 32; KL: 93; TM: 3, 161-174
   function of (see *center, generative*)
   ills resulting from misuse of power of, CH: 47
   law of, is mystery, TM: 161
   life center located in organs of, TM: 22, 162, 163
   physical, MG: 129, 154, 162, 177, 178, 183, 306

generative center, (see *center, generative*)

generosity, P: 89, 108, 132, 133, 136, 152, 153, 156;
   TP: 110

Genesis, ASP: 12, 34, 130; CH: 31-33, 47, 61, 72, 74, 98,
   109; JC: 140, 141, 154, 165; KL: 83; MG: 9, 10,
   11, 13, 14-28, 29, 31, 323, 374; MJ: 11, 12, 32, 73;
   P: 33, 54; TM: 35, 39, 81, 102-105, 146, 167;
   TP: 39, 48, 49, 55, 56, 60, 77, 78, 97, 144, 166;
   TT: 14, 15 (see *allegory; Creation*)
   interpretation of 2d chapter of, P: 33
   six days of creation and "day" of rest in, MG: 11,
   14-28, 31; P: 83-86, 95

genitals, MG: 194

genius, ASP: 52; TM: 136, 137, 139; TP: 44, 116, 117
   and intuition, JC: 48, 113
   and Shakespeare, JC: 49; TM: 139

accessibility of, ASP: 20; TT: 10, 12, 163
affirmation for building consciousness of His presence, TM: 18
all powers of, may become operative in man, JC: 71
and faith, CH: 85-93; JC: 101, 111, 175; MG: 175; P: 42, 49
and freedom, ASP: 19; JC: 23
and Holy Spirit, MJ: 141, 143; TT: 140, 141
and intelligence (see *intelligence, God and*)
and reforming world, ASP: 63; TT: 7, 8
and Sabbath, TM: 112, 113, 116-118
and success, CH: 90; P: 57, 59, 86, 108
as absolute good, KL: 9, 25, 68
as advisor, TT: 12, 13
as all-potential mind, TT: 116, 117
as all-sufficiency in all things, JC: 54, 135; KL: 109
as Cause, TT: 9, 10
as Christ in man, ASP: 76, 77; MJ: 61, 62, 134
as consuming fire, KL: 191
as creator, ASP: 19, 63, 67, 84; CH: 12, 32, 33, 42, 43; JC: 14, 25, 28, 30, 35, 36, 78, 127, 187, 190, 191; KL: 9, 19, 72, 166, 169, 176; TP: 73, 77, 137, 164, 165, 166 (see *Creator; creator*)
as Father, CH: 8, 131, 132; JC: 18, 98, 109, 190; MJ: 47, 60, 73, 89, 90, 130; TP: 88, 162-172
as first in the Trinity, KL: 14
as formless, KL: 14; P: 14, 95, 161
as good, CH: 10, 11, 93; KL: 25, 68
as impartial and just, ASP: 60, 78; CH: 120
as infinite, TT: 9, 10, 104
as intelligence, ASP: 77; JC: 24, 26, 27; KL: 61, 82; TM: 131, 163; TP: 49, 94, 170; TT: 9-13, 88, 95
as knowable only through mind, JC: 23, 30-32, 34, 35, 73, 74; P: 92, 108
as law, ASP: 127, 128; KL: 131; MJ: 141; P: 58, 59; TP: 47
as law-giver, JC: 58, 59
as life, ASP: 19; JC: 23, 29, 37, 47, 78, 104, 162; KL: 58, 60, 122, 123, 132, 162; MJ: 125, 126; P: 95, 171, 179; TM: 131, 132, 163, 164; TP: 13, 14, 94; TT: 149

as male and female principle, MJ: 73, 74

as man's higher self, TT: 11, 12

as man's provider, ASP: 102; JC: 18, 77, 85, 109, 112, 180

as matter, JC: 27

as Mind, ASP: 93, 99; CH: 11, 14, 15, 18, 42, 56, 67, 81; JC: 30-34, 63; KL: 14; MG: 13, 14, 18, 25; P: 77, 161

as mind, ASP: 19, 93; CH: 92; JC: 30, 32, 34, 68, 143; KL: 14; P: 77, 161; TP: 13, 177

as origin of all, TT: 24, 70

as perfect, CH: 61; TP: 164, 172 (see *perfection, God as*)

as potential unformed will, CH: 111; KL: 157

as power, ASP: 91; CH: 8, 11, 67; JC: 25-28, 67; JC: 25, 27; KL: 25, 68; P: 124; TP: 13, 20, 47, 49, 170; TT: 9, 99

as present in all His creations, JC: 36, 130; MG: 13; TP: 14, 83, 84

as primal cause, CH: 10, 13

as principle, ASP: 18; CH: 9, 112; JC: 34-36, 71, 143, 158, 190, 191; KL: 9, 14, 54, 60, 156, 158, 178; P: 46, 58; TM: 52; TT: 11, 130
  of being, JC: 61

as saving power in man, MG: 95

as silent partner in man's prosperity, KL: 104, 105; MG: 229, 230; TP: 40, 146, 147

as source of all, ASP: 59, 93; KL: 65; MG: 138, 229, 230; TP: 94; TT: 66, 67, 70

as source of all good, CH: 98; JC: 67, 77, 109, 112, 120, 135, 169; KL: 101-105; P: 83, 178, 186 (see *God, as supply*)

as source of strength, KL: 149; MG: 351; TM: 37-39, 123

as spirit, ASP: 9, 34, 59-62, 78, 79, 85, 86, 89, 97, 135, 136; CH: 9, 10, 25, 26, 66, 67, 107; JC: 14, 17, 19, 28, 29, 46, 47, 72-74, 78, 82, 85, 87-99, 185

as Spirit of Mind, TT: 7-9, 97, 98

as "still small voice," JC: 27, 28, 49, 50

as still sustaining man and universe, TP: 71

as substance, CH: 26, 27, 29, 35; KL: 14, 15, 58, 61,

creates through thought, CH: 18, 19

daily "date" (communion) with, ASP: 30, 31; TP: 35, 160, 161

dependence on, as source of prosperity, P: 20, 32, 38, 49, 50, 54, 55, 75, 83, 86, 92, 93, 129, 139, 140, 166

does not dictate to man, CH: 108, 109; JC: 112; MJ: 62

does not form things, JC: 35, 36, 138

does not observe Sabbath, TM: 112, 113

does not recognize or countenance death, MJ: 63

does not rest, KL: 171

does not tempt man to break His law, JC: 68; TM: 163

dreams and, CH: 102, 103

Einstein's views on, TM: 86-88

El-Shaddai as feminine name for, ASP: 98

end of old ideas about man and, JC: 20, 70, 71

everything belongs to, P: 152

expresses attributes only through universe and man, JC: 27, 28, 35, 36

expressing, as man's mission, TT: 99, 100

false impressions of character of, KL: 24, 25, 28, 44, 106, 107

falsely conceived of as a person, KL: 25, 28

finding one's being in, MJ: 150, 151

functions constantly with man, KL: 84

gifts of, to man, MJ: 48; P: 77; TM: 137

glorifying, ASP: 122

grace of, KL: 168, 169

has given all things for man to use as he determines, ASP: 52

has provided for all needs of His creation, P: 161, 186

health and, ASP: 76; JC: 23, 27, 30-32, 47, 53, 80, 124, 142; P: 57; TP: 177; TT: 44

hearing voice of, ASP: 56, 57

how to ask of Him, P: 74, 85

how to contact, MJ: 16; P: 92, 119; TT: 11, 12

how to worship, KL: 123, 143

idealized two planes of consciousness, KL: 176

ideas and, ASP: 93, 94; CH: 11, 15; KL: 53, 144, 167; MG: 228-230; MJ: 125, 126; P: 31, 40, 49, 75, 161; TP: 31, 45, 160, 162, 177

transcendent, KL: 144
tribal, MJ: 141
trust in, CH: 135, 136, 138; JC: 169
understandable by man, CH: 8, 11-14, 62; P: 36, 37
unity with, through Christ, JC: 21, 40, 50, 131 (see *unity, with God*)
walking with, KL: 9
where found, JC: 76, 77; TT: 9 (see *kingdom of God*)
why we must perceive, in the flesh, KL: 20
will of, CH: 18, 19, 77, 111, 112; JC: 91
    for man, ASP: 76; CH: 77; JC: 91, 112; P: 37, 38, 46, 60-62, 68, 111-113, 186; TM: 106, 107; TT: 108
Word of, ASP: 135; CH: 61, 62; KL: 15, 142; MG: 43, 58; TP: 17, 165-168, 174; TT: 66, 68, 118 (see *Word of God*)
word of, MG: 43
working with, TP: 30, 146, 147, 162
works in the stillness, TP: 24
works of, ASP: 18, 19, 67, 68; MJ: 98, 105, 140; TM: 112, 113
works through man to manifest the ideal, CH: 33
worship of, JC: 31, 74, 78-80; MJ: 46
wrong concepts of, JC: 25, 31, 34, 68

Godhead, ASP: 84; CH: 20; KL: 112; TT: 70, 71
    man's relation to, JC: 24

God-image, KL: 49

Godliness, JC: 71

God-man, JC: 71; KL: 130

God-mind, CH: 26, 98, 99; JC: 4, 5, 9, 46, 156, 177, 179, 180, 184, 192; KL: 12, 17, 25; MG: 29, 30; P: 56-57, 64, 65, 102; TM: 131; TP: 12, 14-16, 72, 94, 121, 124, 145, 159; TT: 42, 152
    and man's mind, JC: 40, 41
    and the perfect-man idea, CH: 23, 24, 33, 36, 37
    as creative power, MJ: 59, 60

as Spirit, soul, and body (mind, idea, expression),
   CH: 21, 22
as unchanging, CH: 18
faith in, JC: 15
Jesus' personality submerged in, MJ: 65, 66
man and universe within, as living, acting thoughts,
   CH: 19
man as executive power of, TP: 88
Son as idea in, MJ: 61
spiritual consciousness as faculty relating man to,
   CH: 76
the silence, and prosperity, P: 54-56, 64

Gomorrah, MG: 102, 115, 130, 161-163, 168; TM: 146

good, ASP: 151; MG: 358, 360; TM: 79 (see *evil*)
  absolute, KL: 9, 19
  affirmation for establishing the, P: 60
  affirming the, JC: 115; P: 59, 60; TT: 56, 60
  all is, ASP: 49; TM: 132; TT: 116
  as foundation of all existence, MG: 265
  as reality of God and man, P: 59; TT: 116-118
  error of minimizing, TT: 87
  how to attain, P: 143
  imagination and, CH: 101, 105
  power of, TT: 146
  praise and, CH: 79, 80; KL: 180; P: 82
  seeing the, ASP: 75; CH: 93; P: 169-171; TT: 60, 63,
    93, 116-121
  shepherd, MJ: 100, 101
  superconsciousness is the, ASP: 36
  vs. evil, ASP: 114, 155; JC: 178; KL: 87, 88; MG: 35,
    36, 39, 43, 46, 48, 57, 68, 123, 129, 138, 306; P: 59,
    60; MJ: 36, 150, 151; TM: 41-44, 58, 104; TT: 22,
    39, 40 (see *good, vs. bad*)

Good Friday, KL: 139

goodness, divine, KL: 43, 44
  does not guarantee prosperity, KL: 103

Goshen, MG: 339, 341, 342, 352, 358, 362

gospel, JC: 104; TT: 132, 139-142 (see *Jesus Christ,
    gospel of*)

Gospels, MJ: 12; TT: 133

government, P: 147, 187 (see *Babel*)

grace of God, KL: 104, 168, 169; MG: 138, 290

Grand Canyon, KL: 40

Grand Man, KL: 110, 119

grape juice, MG: 88

gratification, sense, JC: 130; KL: 50

gratitude, JC: 137; MJ: 67, 68; TP: 34, 82 (see *praise*)

grave, ASP: 44, 77, 78

graveclothes, KL: 13; MJ: 168

gravitation, P: 12; TP: 108, 110

gravity, MG: 42; TM: 56

Great Britain, ASP: 114, 115

"great gulf fixed," KL: 87

greatness, (difference between human and divine), JC: 147;
    MJ: 124, 125; TP: 20, 108

Great Physician, JC: 109

greed, ASP: 17; JC: 103; P: 147, 151, 167; TP: 98, 99
    (and zeal) 128; TT: 54, 55

Greeks, CH: 62, 63; MJ: 119; P: 11

grief, MG: 330; MJ: 167-169

grippe, affirmation for healing, TP: 180

ground, MG: 33, 35, 57, 60

growth, CH: 22; P: 140, 178; TP: 4, 158 (see *increase*)
    false, JC: 169
    in mind as well as in earth, ASP: 139, 140
    law of, ASP: 27; KL: 97, 139, 140; MJ: 42; TM: 120

spiritual, ASP: 27, KL: 97, 139, 158; TM: 50, 120, 135

grudge, CH: 138

guidance, divine, ASP: 21, 22, 28, 56, 57, 75, 94, 95, 103, 111, 137, 138; CH: 10, 23, 24, 56, 57, 75, 115; JC: 28, 81, 114, 115, 134, 188, 195, 196; KL: 43-53, 56, 66, 67, 91, 175; MJ: 97, 104, 131; P: 18, 39, 45, 46, 59, 78, 124, 125, 135, 136, 174; TM: 73-77, 88, 115, 116, 122, 154, 155; TP: 49, 51, 52, 87; TT: 15, 97, 102-113, 114, 168 (see *intuition; knowing; superconscious mind; leading; Jesus as guide into Father's kingdom; Scriptures, as guide for daily living*)

gulf, TT: 157

Guni, MG: 351

H

habits, ASP: 75; MG: 162, (necessity of struggle in overcoming) 248; TM: 102; P: 112; TT: 96, 97, 165 (see *thought*)

Hadad, son of Bedad, MG: 288, 289
  son of Ishmael, MG: 206

Hadar, or Hadad, MG: 290

Hades, CH: 123, 124; TM: 173

Hadoram, MG: 106

"had the bag," CH: 58

Hagar, MG: 148, 149, 174, 177-179

Haggi, MG: 347

hair, as symbol of vitality, TM: 37

hairy, MG: 220

halo, CH: 89; KL: 148, 149

Ham, country, MG: 132
  son of Noah, MG: 70, 85, 89, 90, 92, 95

Hamathite, MG: 102

Hamilton, Sir William, TM: 83

Hamlet, (Shakespeare), ASP: 111, 112, 114

Hamor, MG: 265, 266, 269

Hamul, MG: 345

handmaid, MG: 261

hands, MG: 194
  laying on of, ASP: 67

Hanoch, son of Midran, MG: 203

Hanock, son of Reuben, MG: 343

happiness,
  and money, P: 162, 163
  as God's will for men, P: 111
  as natural to man, TP: 133, 173, 174
  depends on our attitude, CH: 89, 90
  how found, ASP: 82; JC: 135, 136, 170, 171; KL: 27,
    41, 42; MG: 175, 184; P: 112, 138, 139, 152, 174;
    TP: 174, 177; TT: 123
  is radiated by man, JC: 73
  not found in sense indulgence, TT: 30, 31
  relation of, to health, JC: 169, 170; KL: 27; P: 57, 59,
    60; TP: 132-134
  serving God in spirit of, MG: 175
  should be cultivated, ASP: 32; CH: 93, 128

Haran, land of, MG: 194, 195, 225, 227, 233, 242, 247,
    248, 254
  son of Terah, MG: 113

hardships, ASP: 95; KL: 118; P: 120

hard times, P: 20, 46, 67, 86, 93, 98, 115, 167, 168, 171,
    172

harmony, JC: 120; KL: 115, 120, 190; MG: 23, 26, 64;
    TT: 152, 182 (see *balance; order; love; unity*)
  affirmations for attainment of, JC: 127, 139; MJ: 27;
    TP: 36, 37
  and the kingdom of heaven, JC: 21
  as affiliated with love, CH: 133-135; KL: 30; P: 65;

TP: 107, 111; TT: 59, 61 (see *love, as harmonizer*)
  as related to health, ASP: 147, 149, 158; CH: 41, 42;
    JC: 17, 54, 139, 170, 171
  as related to prosperity, P: 150
  how attained, CH: 132, 133; JC: 60, 118, 119, 130,
    131, 170, 171, 176; KL: 111, 192, 193; MG: 40;
    TP: 43, 44, 72; TT: 57
  in the home, ASP: 72

Harvard, CH: 40

harvest, ASP: 166

hate, KL: 34, 152; P: 118
  effects of, TT: 20
  vs. love, ASP: 148; P: 109, 118; TT: 152, 153

hatred, MG: 215; MJ: 158
  how to nullify, CH: 132, 137

Havilah, land of, MG: 36, 37
  son of Cush, MG: 96

Hazarmaveth, MG: 106

Hazazon-tamar, MG: 133

Hazo, MG: 186

head, TM: 90, 91
  and faculty of praise, MG: 305, 306
  as seat of intellect, CH: 45, 46, 74, 75; KL: 113; P: 61
  as seat of will, MJ: 162; TM: 59, 62, 159
  crown of, represented as spiritual center, TP: 24
  of gold, ASP: 19
  top of, as seat of I AM, TM: 16
  top of, as seat of spirit, CH: 76; TP: 24

healer, true, MJ: 100
  spiritual, ASP: 67, 127; P: 19

healing, CH: 113; JC: 154-196; KL: 117, 161; TP: 153
(see *faith; health; Jesus, and healing; treatment, metaphysical*)
   absent, JC: 144
   affirmations of, JC: 34, 37, 64-66, 118, 137-139, 142,
      144, 147, 150, 153-155, 157, 159, 161-163, 165,
      167-169, 171, 173, 176-179, 182, 184, 186, 188, 190,
      193, 194; KL: 68, 149, 152, 161, 162, 167, 169, 174;
      TP: 18, 66, 70, 73, 77, 83, 86, 90, 93, 100, 104, 107,
      112, 116, 119, 122, 126, 129, 132, 135
   agents of, ASP: 66, 67
   and faith, ASP: 11, 76, 101, 126, 131; CH: 66, 67;
      JC: 53, 56, 74-76, 80, 101, 103, 105, 156; KL: 4,
      28, 173; MG: 54, 55; TP: 27-32, 105, 152, 153, 155,
      164, 165, 178; TT: 49
   and forgiveness, JC: 5, 58-60
   and hypnotism, CH: 113
   and laughter, JC: 168, 169
   and order, JC: 117, 118
   and peace, JC: 29, 139
   and praise, JC: 57, 137, 153
   and receptivity, JC: 112, 113, 176, 177
   and Shakespeare, ASP: 112, 113
   and the prayer of faith, TP: 27-32
   definition of, JC: 9
   denial, JC: 9, 37, 129; TP: 131, 154, 155
   emotion and thought as cause in disease and, TM: 134
   explanation of, ASP: 11
   faith and, ASP: 11, 131
   happiness promotes, JC: 168, 169
   importance of faith in absent, MJ: 54
   instantaneous, JC: 56, 183
   Jesus (Christ) and, CH: 9-21; JC: 39, 56-58, 89-91, 96,
      103, 104, 109, 154-167, 173, 174, 178-181, 184, 185,
      187, 192-196; KL: 173; MJ: 53-55, 57-60, 172;
      P: 78, 153; TM: 30-32; TP: 76, 101-103, 152, 164,
      165, 168, 169, 173, 174, 177, 178; TT: 93, 113-121,
      143, 172, 173
   joy as factor in, JC: 168-181; TP: 104-106, 132-134
   law of, ASP: 11, 32, 126, 130; JC: 112
   logos and, TP: 164-174

love and, MJ: 117; P: 124
medical science vs. Christ way of, TM: 147, 148, 157
metaphysical, JC: 42, 45, 47, 50, 51, 60, 85, 127, 128
miracle theory of, JC: 3
music and, JC: 49
nature of, JC: 9
no case incurable, ASP: 132
no two cases alike, JC: 85
of Naaman, TP: 148-153
only one force of, TP: 101
origin of power of, JC: 18, 19
Peter and John on, TP: 102
power, JC: 57, 155; KL: 22; TP: 19; TT: 143
reasons for delay in, JC: 117, 176; P: 19, 20, 153-155;
    TT: 39, 44, 96, 97
secret of, KL: 22
singing and, JC: 169-173
spiritual, ASP: 66, 67, 89, 131-133; JC: 56, 63, 64;
    KL: 173, 174; TP: 133; TT: 93, 118-121
tenseness vs. relaxation in, TM: 159-160
through cheerfulness, TP: 104-106, 132-134, 136, 137
through power of word, ASP: 71, 72, 99, 101; CH: 66,
    69, 70; JC: 87, 89-91, 94, 109, 154; KL: 174;
    TP: 164-174; TT: 49, 143, 150 (see *affirmation;
    denial; Logos*)
through praise and thanksgiving, JC: 57, 74, 75,
    137-139; TP: 34, 35
through prayer, ASP: 32, 127; CH: 80, 81; JC: 79, 80;
    KL: 20; TP: 27-32, 177-188
through right thinking, CH: 40, 41, 66, 105; KL: 21,
    22, 48, 49, 161; TT: 147, 148 (see *thought, healing
    forces stirred by*)

health, JC: 100; MG: 63, 64, 224, 235; TP: 95, 177;
    TT: 23, 44, 49, 107, 116, 119, 120, 143, 152-155
    (see *healing; affirmation of health*)
affirmations of, instructions for using, ASP: 71, 72, 99,
    101; TP: 131 (see *healing, affirmations of*)
and diet, ASP: 21, 51, 52; JC: 180
and happiness, JC: 169, 170; KL: 27; P: 57, 59, 60;
    TP: 132-134

113

103
word—power of to produce, ASP: 71, 72; TP: 164-174

hearing, TP: 153 (see ears; *receptivity; mind, hearing, and the*)
  cellular, ASP: 56, 57
  receptivity and, MG: 365, 366; TM: 28, 134, 135; TP: 154
  self-will affects, TM: 108
  Simeon as symbolizing, CH: 72, 73, 76; MG: 236, 275
  Simon as symbolizing, TT: 90, 91
  spiritual vs. physical, ASP: 56, 57; CH: 76; TP: 116-118

heart, CH: 91, 99, 113; P: 154 (see *cardiac plexus*)
  as affected by emotion, JC: 169; TM: 20, 134
  as center of love, P: 102
  as faculty (center) of love, TT: 52, 58, 62, 63
  as seat of love, TM: 16, 20
  as subconscious mind, KL: 91
  brain of the, TM: 90
  disease, CH: 54, 111
  keeping the, KL: 91
  purifying the, KL: 92
  singleness of, KL: 92

heat, ASP: 91; JC: 172; MG: 169; P: 12

heathen, P: 136

Heaven, MG: 17

heaven, ASP: 21, 22, 25, 31, 71, 97; JC: 20, 47, 70, 71, 73, 74, 76, 98, 158; KL: 117, 118, 120; MG: 19, 20; MJ: 37, 174; P: 10-12, 76, 114, 166, 167, 177; TM: 69, 70, 162; TP: 13, 101; TT: 17, 88 (see *faith; kingdom of heaven, new era*)
  a light out of, ASP: 26
  and earth, (see *earth, heaven and*)
  and mind, TT: 31, 32
  as creative Mind, KL: 171

helping others, JC: 114, 136

helpmeet, MG: 40

Heman, MG: 284, 285

Hemdam, MG: 286

Henley, William Ernest (quoted), TP: 162

herbs, ASP: 20; MG: 27
  green, recommended for food, MG: 85

herd, MG: 354

heredity, ASP: 76, 77; CH: 116; JC: 33, 37; KL: 64, 66,
  68; MJ: 89, 90; TP: 183, 184; TT: 80 (see *ancestors*)

Herod, KL: 50, 188; TP: 72

Heth, children of, MG: 189, 191, 204
  son of Canaan, MG: 100

Hezron, son of Perez, MG: 343, 344
  son of Reuben, MG: 343, 344

Hiddekel, MG: 37

high place, MG: 108

high priest, (see *priest, high*)

"highway of the Lord," JC: 134

hills, MG: 192

Hindus, ASP: 161; CH: 10; JC: 90; TT: 172

Hinnom, Valley of, CH: 123 (see *Gehenna; hell*)

Hirah, the Asullamite, MG: 302, 303

history, JC: 88
  of man, ASP: 68, 70, 116
  of the race, ASP: 169
  spiritual (see *man, spiritual history of*)

Hitlers (still alive and to come), ASP: 53

Hittites, MG: 176, 374

Hivites, MG: 101, 266, 277, 284

hoarding, JC: 68; KL: 102; P: 16, 17, 22, 52, 53, 90,
  128, 152, 159, 160, 164, 165, 166, 167, 168, 169,
  171

Hobah, MG: 135, 136

holiness, KL: 160; TP: 19, 20

Holy City, KL: 34, 147, 176, 188

Holy Communion, KL: 192, TP: 69

Holy Ghost, TT: 68, 70, 73, 106, 107, 135, 140 (see
  Ghost; Holy Spirit; Spirit of Truth)

holy ground, KL: 191; TM: 122

holy men, P: 10
  and women, JC: 73

Holy Mother, TP: 5

holy of holies, KL: 11; JC: 135, 136; TP: 5, 24 (see *inner
  chamber*)

Holy Spirit, KL: 12, 17, 18, 173; MG: 178; MJ: 128,
  129; P: 48; TP: 53, 69; TT: 71, 101 (see *Holy
  Ghost; Word of God; see man, Holy Spirit and*)

119

humility, KL: 51; MJ: 126, 127; TT: 92, 93

Hupham, MG: 350 (see *Huppim*)

hurry, JC: 121; P: 34

husband, MG: 55; TP: 34

Husham, MG: 289

Hushim, MG: 351

husks, KL: 133

Huxley, Thomas Henry, CH: 30

Hydesville, New York, ASP: 111 (see *Fox sisters*)

Hygeia, JC: 182

hypnotism, CH: 105, 113;
  JC: 46, 160; MJ: 101, 102; TM: 109; TT: 36

hypocrisy, TP: 186

I

symbolized by Jesus, KL: 189
symbolized in Isaac, KL: 82
unlimited in capacity, KL: 56, 57
withdrawal of, MG: 372, 373
without limit capacity, KL: 56

I-am-age, CH: 98, 99

I AM THAT I AM, JC: 141; KL: 145; MJ: 91, 92;
    TM: 54

Idea, Jesus Christ as, KL: 53

idea (s), ASP: 87-97; CH: 46, 48, 74, 75; JC: 48, 49, 90;
    MG: 263, 350; P: 98; TM: 125, 126; TT: 173 (see
    angels; Trinity)
  all things exist as, ASP: 50; CH: 14, 15, 44, 45, 103;
    MG: 32. 33
  and consciousness, MG: 116, 117, 263
  and expression, CH: 16, 34, 38, 96; JC: 113, 114, 121,
    122, 179, 180; MG: 23; P: 26-36, 48, 49, 50, 56;
    TP: 96, 97; TT: 15, 170
  and ideas, CH: 44, 46, 99; JC: 40, 41, 72, 75
  and faith, CH: 90; JC: 35, 101, 114, 175; KL: 119;
    TM: 28, 29; TP: 32
  and health, JC: 30, 31
  and laws governing their manifestation, ASP: 37, 99,
    100, 104, 140, 144, 153, 154; CH: 32, 34, 38, 43;
    JC: 175; KL: 172, 173, 178 (see manifestation,
    idea(s) and mind, also see mind, idea and)
  and order, JC: 130
  and Principle, P: 57
  and prosperity, P: 88, 89, 92, 109, 124, 125, 156, 157,
    167
  and wealth, P: 77, 94
  and word, (see word, and idea)
  are brought into being through mind of man, ASP: 37,
    120, 139, 140, 141; CH: 32, 33, 34; P: 56, 64, 65,
    68, 80, 81, 83, 98, 117, 123, 155, 176; TM: 125;
    TP: 124; TT: 16, 170, 176
  are made visible through words, TP: 168; TT: 176

as angels, ASP: 45, 46
as catching, JC: 136; KL: 172; P: 40, 148
as directing and controlling power, MG: 21
as eternal realities, P: 43
as food of faith—thinking faculty, KL: 119
as free heaven, KL: 118
as generator of thought and word, P: 12, 13, 26, 28
as Jehovah God, TT: 14, 24
as key to problems of life, CH: 13, 14, 31, 32, 77, 101
as Logos, (see *idea, as Word*)
as means of communication between God and man,
　JC: 32, 33, 35, 36; KL: 11
as seeds, ASP: 135, 139, 140; TT: 106, 108
as Son, KL: 14-18, 173; TT: 134
as sons and daughters of God, TM: 52, 53
as source of substance, KL: 11, 184; P: 22, 24, 67, 68,
　73, 108; TM: 122
as source of things, JC: 17, 18, 35, 36, 40, 41, 109, 175,
　178; P: 28-36, 48, 49, 50, 56, 75, 76, 77, 78, 95, 160;
　TM: 34, 35, 72, 122; TP: 96
as symbols, TM: 77
as Word, ASP: 136; CH: 61; KL: 165; MJ: 11, 12, 76
body carried in mind as, CH: 34; JC: 186
bring forth after their kind, MG: 19, 24; TM: 143, 144
can be made manifest, ASP: 67; JC: 113; P: 37, 161,
　162
catching, KL: 172
character of, KL: 47; P: 180, 181
Christ as divine, KL: 165; MJ: 11, 61, 124; P: 85
conception of, MG: 27
creative, MG: 39
development of, ASP: 43; CH: 96; JC: 113, 175;
　KL: 16, 46, 47, 154, 155, 165; MG: 45, 115, 117,
　335
divine, ASP: 45, 68, 76, 77; CH: 13, 63; MG: 12,
　20-22, 24, 25, 27, 33, 35, 50, 52, 71, 113, 317; P: 85
　(see *seed*)
Divine Mind deals only with, MG: 17, 18
every manifest thing representative of, P: 32, 33, 50;
　CH: 103
every word has its root in an, TP: 90, 91

of God, JC: 161; KL: 92

of health, KL: 48

of man to be adjusted to those of Divine Mind, ASP: 43;
  KL: 13; P: 31, 150, 151

perfect-man, CH: 20, 23, 24, 33, 36, 37

physical body carried in mind as, JC: 186

power of, CH: 38; JC: 87, 149, 156; KL: 80; MG: 21;
  P: 29; TM: 65; TT: 28, 29, 41

prayer makes man master of creative, KL: 10

reaction of mind to, JC: 90, 94, 95, 129, 130

realization of an, TP: 19, 29, 39

realm of, JC: 71, 90; KL: 11, 49, 147, 156; P: 35, 99,
  186, 187

rule of man, TP: 64, 65

should be accepted only with caution, JC: 119

should be expressed in action, JC: 113, 114

Son as, ASP: 99

soul of man fed by, P: 80, 81

spiritual, JC: 51, 74, 96, 97, 102, 103; MG: 73, 203,
  228, 255; MJ: 51, 73, 74

superconscious as realm of divine, ASP: 36

symbolized by fish, KL: 172; MG: 100

symbolized by Ithran, MG: 287

symbolized by Sidon, MG: 100

tendency to cling to old, MG: 373, 374; P: 178

thinking faculty of man as formative vehicle of God's,
  ASP: 93, 94, 104

youth as an, MJ: 110, 111; P: 37

ideal(s)

as symbolizing heaven, ASP: 43

how to give it form, JC: 113, 132, 133; KL: 22, 23;
  MG: 238, 239; P: 65, 66, 178; TM: 121; TT: 119,
  126

vs. the manifest, ASP: 45; CH: 33, 103, 104, 132, 133;
  KL: 22, 25, 63, 176; MG: 226; TT: 68

idealization, TT: 117

identity, CH: 46; TM: 48, 53, 100; TT: 83 (see *Christ,
  man's identity with*)

body as means of, ASP: 118
divine, of spirit in man, ASP: 127, 128; CH: 22, 36, 37;
   MJ: 134
endures, KL: 94, 95, 97, 98
establishing one's, with Christ, ASP: 23; TM: 50, 51
experience develops personal, CH: 55
formed by Christ's attributes, KL: 110
has its center in head, TM: 48
I AM, ASP: 123
man's spiritual, ASP: 32, 102-104, 122; P: 98
thought as, CH: 50

"I die daily," CH: 59

idols, P: 136, 182; TT: 103 (see *Scriptures, man's tendency to make idol of*)

ignorance, CH: 80, 113, 114; KL: 57, 96; MJ: 90, 100,
   131
   keeps man from his own, KL: 55
   penalty of, ASP: 87, 88

ills, (see *sickness; poverty*)
   bodily, MG: 122, 172
   financial, P: 117-130, 156-158
   mental, cause of, ASP: 147, 148; CH: 64, 65; JC: 31,
      53, 104, 135, 136, 168; MG: 172; TM: 59, 146-151
      (see *sin, all ills of humanity are result of*)
      how to heal, CH: 46, 47, 64, 65; JC: 16-19, 31, 53,
         104, 105, 134, 135, 168-181; MG: 122; TM: 59

ill temper, JC: 103

illumination, spiritual, ASP: 154, 155; KL: 170, 171;
   MG: 300; P: 117; TM: 88, 89, 90, 91; TP: 49, 50,
   145, 146
   affirmation for, P: 35, 36
   secret of Paul's, ASP: 27, 28

illusion, world of, KL: 63, 64, 89

image, ASP: 19 (see *image and likeness; thought, images*)
    and expression, ASP: 47, 120, 121; JC: 113, 114, 178;
        P: 40, 76-79, 94, 95, 100; TM: 71, 72, 80;
        TP: 70-72
    as idea, ASP: 135; MG: 270; P: 76, 77; TM: 77

image and likeness, ASP: 18, 100, 117, 118, 130, 135,
    151, 152; CH: 19, 26, 32, 98, 108; JC: 47, 154;
    KL: 17, 49, 59, 60, 62, 83, 89, 155, 176; MG: 78;
    P: 160; TM: 71, 99, 100, 104, 163; TP: 55 (see
    *Christ, as image and likeness; man, as image and like-
    ness*)

imagination, ASP: 21; CH: 96, 105; P: 94, 95; TT: 15
    (see *daydreams; image and expression; Bartholomew;
    Jacob; Joseph; Tiras*)
    affirmation for developing, KL: 155
    and abundance, P: 88, 177
    and demonstration, (see *demonstration of Truth, love
    and*)
    and faith, JC: 108, 109; P: 49, 76, 91
    and manifestation, (see *manifestation, imagination and*)
    and prosperity, P: 40, 49, 66, 67, 81, 82, 84, 85, 88, 94,
    95, 96, 100, 114, 115
    and regeneration, TM: 71-82, 102, 103, 141
    and sense consciousness, MG: 73, 74, 390, 391
    and supply, MG: 329, 330; P: 94; TT: 55
    and understanding, MJ: 22; TM: 100, 101
    and wealth, P: 95, 96
    and will, MG: 359; P: 77, 78; TM: 100
    as daughter of God, TM: 53
    as faculty for increasing and molding, CH: 96-106;
    JC: 50, 51; MG: 244-247, 293, 321, 355; MJ: 11;
    P: 49, 84, 91, 96; TM: 71; TT: 70, 71, 116
    as faculty required for shaping thought, CH: 98, 99
    as measure of man's accomplishment, CH: 96;
    MG: 301; TT: 99
    as related to visions and dreams, TM: 74-79
    as third step in creation, MG: 18, 19
    as transformer of character, CH: 105, 106
    as used by Jesus, P: 78, 79

impurity, ASP: 104; TT: 153, 154

inanimate objects, filled with infinite life, P: 140

incarnated in the flesh, Jesus Christ, ASP: 24

incarnation, ASP: 32, 122; KL: 26; MJ: 35, 36, 137 (see
    Jesus; reincarnation)
  of Christ, KL: 131

incense, P: 44

income, living within one's, P: 125 (see *tithing*)

increase, P: 47 (see *blessing, and law of increase; substance;
    vitality*)
  and Christ substance, MJ: 177, 178
  gratitude, thanksgiving, and praise in relation to,
    JC: 139; MJ: 67-70
  Joseph as representing faculty of, MG: 293, 320, 321
  law of, P: 46, 47, 81, 82, 84, 100, 105, 106, 108, 109,
    140, 143, 152, 186; KL: 101

incurables, no, ASP: 132, 133

indecision, TP: 129

India, ASP: 114
  and the priesthood, CH: 21; P: 90
  Empire of, ASP: 115

indigestion, TM: 134

indignation, righteous, CH: 125; TP: 107

individuality, CH: 16, 36; KL: 145; MG: 45; P: 107;
    TT: 135, 167, 177, 178 (see *I AM; personality; con-
    sciousness, individual*)
  vs. personality, JC: 69

industry, TP: 89

indwelling Father, (see *Father, indwelling; Jesus and indwelling Father*)

inefficiency, P: 177

inertia, MJ: 137

inferiority complex, ASP: 63; KL: 66, 67; TP: 78; TT: 142 (see *personality*)
   treatment for, JC: 37

Infinite Mind, (see *Mind, Infinite*)

influence, Personal, JC: 147

influenza, affirmation for healing, TP: 180

Ingersoll, Robert (quoted), KL: 24; MG: 22; TP: 21

inharmony, ASP: 148; P: 104, 123, 149, 159; TT: 162

"inherit the kingdom," ASP: 46

inheritance, KL: 144; MJ: 38
   affirming one's divine, ASP: 76
   man's spiritual, CH: 36; P: 185; TM: 64
   mental, MJ: 33
   plenty is man's, from God, P: 59-69

initiative, KL: 137; TP: 155

injustice, CH: 125, 126, 129; MG: 259; TP: 107, 181

"inner chamber," P: 151 (see *silence; upper room*)
   and prayer, CH: 81; TP: 3, 5, 16, 17, 24, 25, 81, 177

inner eye, KL: 12

inner, the, P: 146, 147 (see *outer, the*)

innocence, P: 184; TT: 107, 108, 136

inoculation, TM: 147, 148, 157

insect, TP: 30; TT: 59

insight, spiritual, ASP: 20

inspiration, ASP: 20, 22; CH: 8, 10; JC: 82, 100, 111;
    KL: 173; MG: 34, 37, 50, 76, 77, 106, 139, 223,
    238, 241, 313, 314, 317, 342, 370; MJ: 47, 48, 49;
    TM: 45, 54, 74, 84; TP: 17, 127; TT: 9, 99, 102,
    104, 114, 130, 138, 139 (see *intuition*)
  vs. intellectual reasoning, JC: 111

installment plan, P: 125

instinct, JC: 42; MG: 224; P: 72; TM: 116

institutions, established, JC: 20

instruction, source of, ASP: 21

intangible, the, ASP: 50

integrity, JC: 103, 115

intellect, ASP: 89; CH: 75; JC: 42, 111; KL: 45;
    MG: 19, 55, 68, 98, 106, 202, 203, 210, 267, 303;
    MJ: 33, 41, 42, 105; P: 45; TT: 10, 139, 159 (see
    intuition; Jacob; love; Pharisees; wisdom)
  and belief, CH: 85, 86
  and demonstration, JC: 111
  and faith, CH: 86, 87; TM: 18
  and lust for power, KL: 59
  and microbes, TT: 14-27
  and realization, TP: 25
  and Spirit, MJ: 41, 42, 49, 50, 58, 80, 81, 86, 87, 91;
    TT: 22, 89
  and Truth seeking, JC: 106
  and wisdom, CH: 97; MG: 93; TT: 21-23
  arguing, MJ: 91, 102, 113
  as Adam man, TM: 153; TT: 15, 16, 18, 21

as another name for God, ASP: 77
as light, JC: 37; MG: 16, 114; TP: 75, 119, 120, 153,
154; TT: 69
as Son of God, TM: 53
centers of, CH: 38; MG: 117
Father as omnipresent, CH: 11; MJ: 86, 146; TT: 72
God and, ASP: 77; JC: 26, 27; KL: 61; MG: 15, 131,
206, 207; P: 35; TM: 53, 131, 163; TP: 94, 144;
TT: 26
light representing, MJ: 31
man as outlet of omnipresent, CH: 22
matter and, ASP: 92; JC: 40
Mind as fount of, ASP: 90
mind as source of, CH: 44; JC: 40, 78, 121, 122, 191;
TT: 10
omnipresent, KL: 45, 59, 132; P: 45, 46
one directive, in universe, TP: 98
realm of ideas as source of, KL: 49
spiritual, TP: 15
thought carries, JC: 138
two types of, JC: 24

interest, P: 127

interpretation, metaphysical, CH: 123
Bible, (see *Bible, interpretation of*)
of dreams and visions, TM: 72, 73
Scriptural, (see *Scriptures, interpretation of*)

intervention, divine, ASP: 10

intonation, JC: 164

intuition, ASP: 88, 89; CH: 7, 8, 10, 98, 114; JC: 42, 48,
49, 91, 98, 102; KL: 48, 49, 191; MG: 50, 185, 219,
221, 242, 266, 269; MJ: 24; P: 45, 46, 99; TM: 20,
45, 47, 67, 77, 85-86, 88, 90, 122; TP: 50, 127, 130,
151, 154, 155; TT: 71, 73, 113, 115, 146, 174 (see
genius; knowing)
and mind, ASP: 89
and woman, ASP: 88, 89; MG: 50; MJ: 27

as instinct of animal soul, JC: 42

Einstein on, JC: 49, 50
knowing through, CH: 114
vs. intellect, TM: 44, 45, 85, 86, 89

invention, ASP: 52, 61, 63, 64, 65; P: 99; TM: 135, 136

investment, P: 171

invisible, the, ASP: 50, 134; KL: 102; P: 27, 28; TP: 30

invocation, TP: 183

involution, MG: 14, 25, 26, 323
    of mind, preceding evolution of matter, TM: 121

Irad, MG: 62

Isaac, KL: 78, 79, 80, 82; MG: 141, 144, 148, 149, 151,
        152, 155, 160, 174-177, 183, 185, 189, 194, 195,
        199, 200, 201, 204, 205, 208, 209, 211, 213, 214,
        216, 218, 223, 276, 323, 363; MJ: 34, 89
    as I AM, TP: 139-143
    as connecting link between Abraham (faith) and Israel
        (manifestation), MG: 217
    as symbolizing joy, MG: 208, 213, 216; MJ: 139
    as symbolizing peace, MG: 216

Isaiah, ASP: 43, 54, 162, 163; JC: 81; KL: 39, 40;
        TM: 26, 82, 88, 92; TP: 78, 134

Iscah, MG: 114

Ishbak, MG: 202

Ishmael, MG: 149, 155, 177, 179, 207, 226

Ishmaelites, MG: 226, 298

Ishvah, MG: 347, 348

Isis, TT: 99 (see *Osiris*)

Israel, MJ: 21, 22, 34
   children of, P: 155-156, 180-184 (see *Jacob*)
   king of, TP: 149, 150
   man, MG: 151, 259, 261, 265, 274, 362
   nation of, MG: 124
   twelve tribes of, ASP: 38

Israelites, ASP: 81; JC: 140, 147; KL: 37, 79, 104;
   MG: 202, 287, 299, 325, 352; MJ: 47; TP: 141

Issachar, MG: 241, 275, 346, 367

Ithran, MG: 286, 287

I will, CH: 33, 34; JC: 24; TP: 17; TT: 24, 30
   as Adam (manifest man), CH: 33, 34, 38

I WILL BE THAT I WILL BE, CH: 109

J

Jabal, MG: 63, 64

Jabbok, MG: 261

Jachin, MG: 344

Jacob, JC: 71; MG: 369; MJ: 34, 44, 47, 89 (see *dreams;
     intellect; Israel*)
  and death, MG: 360, 361, 363, 371
  and Esau, TP: 139-147
  and his covenant with God, KL: 84
  and his growth in consciousness, KL: 83, 84, 86;
     MG: 189, 223-276, 352, 355, 358, 371
  and prosperity, MG: 246
  and tithing, KL: 84, 85, 104; MG: 229; P: 131;
     TP: 146, 147
  and understanding, MG: 228, 259
  as idea of Truth, MG: 353
  as intellect, MG: 209-212, 218-221, 223, 225, 230, 232,
     233, 244-247, 254-259, 261, 262, 265, 267, 272, 278,
     279, 294, 300, 301, 358
  as representative of I AM, MG: 237, 238, 297, 323-327,
     330-332, 337, 339, 341, 342, 352, 359-363; TM: 97
  as spiritual insight, MG: 223
  as supplanter, MG: 211, 231
  as symbol of the I AM, TM: 97
  blessing as practiced by, (see *blessing, as practiced by
     Jacob*)
  blessing of, KL: 78, 79; MG: 223, 229, 258, 259, 362,
     364, 366; TP: 139-142
  dreams of, CH: 101, 102; KL: 83, 84; MG: 227, 228,
     247; TT: 136 (see *visions, of Jacob*)
  experiences with tithing, KL: 85, 104; MG: 209-212,
     218-221, 223, 225, 230, 232, 233, 244-247, 254-259,
     261, 262, 264, 265, 267, 269, 272, 278, 279, 294,
     300, 301, 358, 372-374

represents the mind, KL: 79 (see *Jacob, as intellect*)
story of receiving Isaac's blessing, KL: 78; MG: 211, 231
twelve sons of, as twelve faculties of man, CH: 72-76, 101, 102, 130, 131; MG: 231-243, 354, 364-370 (see *faculties*)
"wrestling" of, with angel, MG: 258

Jacob's ladder, KL: 83

Jacob's well, MG: 44, 47, 49

Jah, MG: 347

Jahleel, MG: 346

Jahzeel, MG: 351

Jalam, MG: 277, 278

James, JC: 79, 178, 179; MG: 16; P: 75-76; TP: 27, 60, 120, 121
instruction to purify heart, KL: 92
judgment, ASP: 152, 153; CH: 92
son of Alphaeus, MG: 242; TM: 15, 22, 110, 129 (see *order*)
son of Zebedee, ASP: 40, 152; CH: 92; KL: 117; P: 45; TM: 16, 19, 20, 45, 49, 133, 167; TT: 53 (see *discrimination; judgment; justice; wisdom*)
symbol of power of justice, KL: 11
the Just, JC: 79, 178; KL: 92; MG: 16; P: 75, 76; TP: 27, 60, 120

Jamin, MG: 344

Japan, ASP: 15

Japanese, JC: 90; TT: 173

Japanese earthquake, ASP: 29

Japheth, MG: 70, 85, 89, 90, 92 (see *Tiras*)

Jared, MG: 69

Javan, MG: 93, 95

Jazer, MG: 351

jealousy, ASP: 104; CH: 126, 127, 137; KL: 65, 152;
    TP: 178; TT: 20
  allusion to, JC: 46

Jeans, Sir James (quoted), ASP: 14, 15, 169
  "The Mysterious Universe," MJ: 69; P: 14; TP: 97, 98;
    TT: 41

Jebusite, MG: 101

Jegar-sahadutha, MG: 252

Jehovah, ASP: 20; JC: 139, 154, 156, 182; MG: 62, 148,
    160-162, 167; P: 184, 185, 228; TM: 84; TP: 24,
    121, 130, 144, 145, 146, 150; TT: 136 (see *Christ; I
    AM: Jehovah God*)
  and Christ, JC: 155, 156
  and Christianizing of all nations, MG: 169, 170
  ark of, MG: 77
  as active representative of Divine Mind, MG: 38, 39
  as Christ, ASP: 100, 101; JC: 155, 157, 182, 183;
    KL: 21, 98, 130, 132, 153
  as Father, ASP: 10 (see *Father, Jehovah as*)
  as God's idea of man, KL: 15
  as Holy Spirit, TT: 135
  as I AM, ASP: 80; CH: 109; JC: 14, 122, 123, 141,
    157, 164; KL: 15; MG: 12, 28, 30, 32, 34; TM: 54,
    103; TP: 145, 150; TT: 76, 77, 157
    I AM THAT I AM, TM: 54; TP: 136, 137
  as image-and-likeness, MG: 78
  as individual I AM, JC: 158
  as law, MG: 60, 61, 310, 311
  as Lord, JC: 122

as Lord God, CH: 109; TT: 119
as name of supermind in man, TP: 136, 137
as tribal God of Israelites, JC: 141, 142, 148; TM: 106;
TP: 137; TT: 135, 136
as word, ASP: 54, 55; JC: 154, 155; KL: 153; TP: 18,
77
held in silence, KL: 170
as universal Mind, MG: 58, 59
calling upon name of, MG: 65, 66
conscience as voice of, MG: 51, 52
effects of thoughts opposed to commandments of,
ASP: 81
man, TM: 54
promises of, KL: 161, 180; MG: 151-153
relation between Christ mind and mind of, ASP: 100,
101
spiritually one with the Father, TM: 106
temple of, ASP: 120, 121

Jehovah God, JC: 154, 178; MG: 41, 49, 50; TP: 52, 64,
97 (see *conscience; Divine Mind; Elohim God; I AM;
Jehovah; man, spiritual*)
ark of, MG: 77
as active representative of Divine Mind, MG: 38, 39
as executive power of Elohim, JC: 141; MG: 28
as forming man, JC: 187; MG: 54
as I AM, CH: 33, 34; MG: 57
as image-and-likeness man, MG: 78
as infinite mind in expression, TT: 11
as law, MG: 60, 61, 310, 311
as name for Being, JC: 158; TT: 14, 15
calling the name of, MG: 65, 66
conscience as voice of, MG: 51, 52
promises of, MG: 151-153
triune aspects of, MG: 157-159, 165

Jehovah-jireh, JC: 141; MG: 184; P: 40; TM: 26;
TP: 137

Jehovah man, vs. Adam man, TM: 35

Jehovah-rapha, JC: 123, 141, 142, 155

Jehovah-shalom, JC: 141, 142

Jehovah-shammah, JC: 164; P: 40; TP: 136, 137

Jemuel, MG: 344

Jerah, MG: 106

Jeremiah, MG: 221

Jerico, walls of, ASP: 54

Jerusalem, ASP: 59, 66, 84, 121, 144, 145; KL: 37;
    MJ: 28, 46, 80, 118, 158, 172, 181
  as representing peace, MJ: 56, 114
  as symbol of great nerve center, KL: 34
  as symbol of love center, KL: 34
  as symbol of peace, KL: 188, 189; MJ: 56, 114
  as symbol of spirituality, ASP: 54, 66, 144, 145;
    MJ: 56, 109 (see New Jerusalem)

Jesus, KL: 119; MJ: 28, 77; P: 44, 71, 179; TP: 11, 77,
    78, 94; TM: 7, 35, 36, 99, 105 (see Christ; Father; I
    AM; Jesus Christ; Son; son)
  alive in body electricity, ASP: 22-24
  alive now in spiritual ethers, ASP: 22-25; JC: 11, 12,
    83, 84, 110
  as adept in scientific prayer, TP: 25, 26 (see prayer,
    Jesus and)
  and abundance, (see abundance, Jesus and)
  and abundant life, ASP: 66, 67; JC: 105
  and body redemption, ASP: 122, 131, 147, 149, 157,
    158; JC: 13-15, 146, 147, 158, 159
  and casting out demons, TM: 66
  and centurion's faith, CH: 66, 67
  and Christianizing of all nations, MG: 169, 170
  and Comforter, JC: 179, 182, 195; MJ: 81, 134
  and control of elements, TM: 31, 108
  and conversion of Paul, JC: 12

144

and creeds and dogmas, TM: 92, 110-117; TT: 132, 133
  (see *creeds*)
and draught of fishes, MJ: 177, 178
and demonstration of Truth, (see *demonstration of
  Truth, Jesus and*)
and earthly parentage, TT: 80, 81
and ecclesiastical ritualism, TM: 110-116
and evolution, JC: 54, 55
and faith, (see *faith, Jesus and*)
and fasting, KL: 4; MJ: 51; TP: 105 (see *fasting*)
and feeding of the multitude, P: 84, 91, 100, 159 (see
  Jesus, miracles of)
and first birth, CH: 25, 26, 73 (see *birth, first*)
and freedom of individual, MJ: 140
and Galileans' unbelief, MJ: 52
and greatest commandment, TP: 58, 113 (see *Jesus, and
  love*)
and healing, ASP: 11, 14, 67, 76, 126, 149; JC: 3-5, 41,
  45, 56, 60, 79, 103, 104, 105; KL: 173; MJ: 51, 53,
  54, 60, 98, 109, 110, 171, 172; TM: 157; TP: 152,
  153, 164, 165 (see *Jesus, miracles of; Jesus, healing
  methods of*)
and higher astronomy, ASP: 161, 162
and high Truth statements, ASP: 37
and His communion with God in silence, TT: 137, 138
and His demonstration over death, ASP: 143, 145
and His disciples, MJ: 24, 25, 80, 89, 128, 135, 140,
  142, 143, 145, 181, 182; P: 45; TM: 15, 16, 17, 21,
  45, 50, 61, 72, 73, 74, 104, 133, 134, 158; TT: 52-54
and His part in opening man's way into glory, MJ: 149,
  150
and His warning against the idea of personal appearance
  of Christ, ASP: 171
and Holy Spirit, ASP: 41; JC: 155; MJ: 136 (see *Holy
  Spirit*)
and human kinship, CH: 131, 132
and indwelling Father, ASP: 130; JC: 187, 190;
  TM: 54; TT: 35-37 (see *Father, indwelling*)
and inner realm of mind. P: 34-35, 80
and Judas, CH: 58, 59
and judgment, CH: 121, 122, 123, 125

and judgment day, TM: 44
and kingdom of God, (see *Jesus, and kingdom of heaven;
kingdom, of God, of heaven*)
and kingdom of God; also kingdom of heaven, CH: 11,
13-15, 66, 67, 90, 91, 100, 101; JC: 99, 134, 135,
138, 139, 148, 150, 165, 166; P: 11, 12, 16; TM: 8,
9; TT: 31, 34, 36, 126-131 (see *Jesus, and kingdom
of the heavens*)
and kingdom of the heavens, ASP: 9, 16, 22, 40, 56, 58,
85, 170, 141; TM: 86; TP: 163 (see *kingdom of the
heavens*)
and law, ASP: 161, 162, 168; KL: 88; TM: 48
and law of equal distribution of supply, P: 125-128
and law of prosperity, P: 34, 47, 48, 60, 63, 64, 66, 88,
90, 91, 109, 144, 186, 187 (see *law, of prosperity*)
and law of thought affinity, MJ: 135; TP: 101, 102
and life, ASP: 66, 77; CH: 58, 105, 144, 145, 146, 156,
157, 162, 163, 173, 174; JC: 146, 173, 174;
KL: 132; TT: 148, 149, 150
and light, (see *light, Jesus and*)
and loaves and fishes, MJ: 69, 74; P: 46, 47, 84 (see
loaves and fishes)
and Logos, TP: 169, 170
and Lord's Prayer, JC: 67, 68, 83, 109; TP: 3
and love, ASP: 148, 149; CH: 135, 137, 138; KL: 33,
34; MJ: 117; P: 65, 70, 109, 110; TM: 59; TP: 113;
TT: 51
and man born blind, MJ: 96-99
and man's specific work in world, ASP: 95, 96
and material things, JC: 81, 97 (see *materiality, Jesus
showed how to be free from*)
and meaning of the cross, TM: 70, 156
and mind, ASP: 40, 147, 148; JC: 186-190; MJ: 180;
P: 176; TT: 124, 125
and money, P: 113, 186, 187
and Nathanael, MJ: 21, 22
and new birth, JC: 85 (see *birth, new*)
and new race, CH: 90, 91; TM: 3, 4
and Nicodemus, MJ: 33, 34, 37
and obedience to God's will, CH: 33; TT: 91, 92
and order, P: 84

and overcoming, MG: 231, 232, 258; TM: 67, 68, 69;
TP: 110, 111, 136; TT: 25, 166 (see *overcoming*)
   of death, JC: 90, 91, 132, 133, 146, 162; MJ: 92, 93,
      172, 173, 175; P: 37; TP: 4, 6, 69, 88, 89, 175;
      TM: 9, 91, 92, 170, 172-174
   of hard conditions, TT: 25
and parable of Lazarus and rich man, TT: 155, 158, (see
   Jesus, parables of)
and parable of loaves and fishes, ASP: 102 (see *Jesus,
   parables of*)
and parable of seed, ASP: 59 (see *Jesus, parables of*)
and Paul, ASP: 26, 27
and peace, JC: 21, 142; MJ: 171
and persecution, MJ: 142, 161
and Pharisees, ASP: 90, 100, 103, 145; CH: 23;
   MJ: 77, 78, 80; TM: 110
and power, JC: 145; KL: 187; P: 48; TM: 30, 61, 65,
   141 (see *power, Jesus and*)
   of I AM, TT: 25
   of spoken word, ASP: 30, 37, 67, 148, 149; JC: 5, 9,
      15, 47, 88, 94, 97, 99, 133, 144, 154, 161; MJ: 62,
      76, 82, 83, 93, 135; P: 112, 148, 176; TM: 30, 62,
      83; TP: 164, 165
and power of words, TP: 73, 74; TM: 39
and prayer, ASP: 12, 126; JC: 12, 13, 57, 67, 68, 69,
   70, 77, 78, 83, 84, 99, 175; KL: 65, 72; MJ: 150;
   P: 47; TM: 107, 108; TP: 3, 4, 5, 6, 16, 25, 26, 28,
   29, 63, 81, 85, 101, 105, 157; TT: 137, 168
and presence of God, TP: 5, 14, 15
and race consciousness, JC: 146, 147, 159, 167; TP: 22,
   64, 65, 68, 69, 101; TT: 164-168 (see *consciousness,
   race*)
and race, human, (see *race, human, Jesus Christ and*)
and radiant body, ASP: 22
and raising of dead, CH: 34, 35; TT: 38, 42, 45-47, 118
   (see *dead, raising the*)
and raising of Lazarus, MJ: 107-112
and reform, P: 147, 148 (see *reform*)
and regeneration, ASP: 42; CH: 38, 39; JC: 10, 11, 52,
   83, 84, 94, 110, 146, 162, 184, 185, 193; KL: 163;
   MG: 35, 48, 49, 71, 154; TM: 3, 119, 120, 158;

148

as advanced soul, ASP: 22

as "a king," MJ: 158

as allegory of man's development from natural to spiritual, CH: 73, 74

as appointed head of race, JC: 19

ascension of, through body regeneration, JC: 72, 73, 83, 132

as center of faith, ASP: 10, 40

as channel for grace and truth, KL: 169

as charged with spiritual substance, P: 21, 78, 79

as Christ (savior), ASP: 100, 122; JC: 9-11; KL: 111-115, 130-135; MJ: 15, 41, 48, 80, 84-87, 92, 114, 122, 128, 149, 156; TP: 150

as continuous working factor in civilization, KL: 164

as demonstrator and teacher of mind laws, JC: 5, 39, 42, 54, 79, 95, 96, 99, 142, 147, 149, 156, 157, 162, 184, 187

as demonstrator of God's law, ASP: 147; TT: 43, 52, 111, 118, 144, 168, 170

as demonstrator of highest type of embodiment, ASP: 122, 152, 168, 169, 171

as demonstrator of imperishable body, ASP: 11; JC: 83, 145, 146, 159, 184, 185 (see *body*)

as demonstrator of spiritual strength, TM: 37

as direct descendant of Judah, MG: 366, 367

as dynamic life-giving force, TM: 158; TP: 64, 65, 68, 69, 75, 102, 103

as enigma to worldly-wise, TT: 71, 72

as every man's name, TM: 47

as example to human family, JC: 191; MJ: 39, 124, 162, 163; P: 179

as executive of spiritual principle, TP: 87

as fearless of disease, JC: 57

as "first fruit" of earth's first age, ASP: 131

as fulfillment of the law (affirmation), P: 70, 71

as genius, TM: 136, 137; TT: 67

as God manifest, MJ: 130; TP: 56

as God's idea of man, MJ: 3

as God vs. Jesus as man, ASP: 167, 168

as greatest genius, TM: 23, 136-137

as guide into Father's kingdom, ASP: 167, 168; JC: 152, 167; TM: 73, 74; TP: 90, 101-103; TT: 35, 36, 43, 126-131, 141, 142, 161, 178
as herald of new set of laws, CH: 90, 91
as I AM, or central entity, ASP: 156; CH: 109; JC: 156, 158; KL: 180, 189, 195; MJ: 24-27, 44, 49, 57, 68, 69, 87, 103, 105, 107, 110, 128, 133, 134, 153, 155, 168; TM: 16, 28; TT: 25
as joint heir to kingdom, KL: 27
as Lamb of God, MJ: 18, 19
as life and light of men, TP: 60, 61, 75, 119
as light of the world, KL: 127, 128
as living word, MJ: 65, 66, 93
as Lord, TT: 47
as man, ASP: 167-168; CH: 30; MJ: 109
as master and servant, TP: 56-59
as master mason, ASP: 120, 121
as Messiah, ASP: 166
as one of God-men, KL: 130
as only begotten Son, CH: 25; TM: 40, 118
as our Elder Brother, TP: 64
as our teacher and helper, KL: 164; TP: 12, 13, 64, 85
as perfect expression of God-Mind, JC: 9, 69, 156
as product of former cycle of time, MJ: 149
as prophet, ASP: 164
as psychologist, KL: 76
as restorer of life current between God and man, MG: 39
as resurrected Adam, TT: 137, 151
as Savior, ASP: 62; TP: 22-24, 64, 75, 101, 164; TT: 167, 168
as Son-of-God consciousness in man, TM: 44, 118, 119
as Son of God, ASP: 36, 37, 42, 129, 130; TP: 88, 165; TT: 170
as Son of man, P: 32; TP: 88
as spiritual consciousness, TM: 151
as spiritual man, JC: 47; TP: 29
as successful demonstrator of prayer, ASP: 126, 127
as teacher, KL: 36, 41, 57, 73, 89, 149, 164; TM: 7, 45, 73, 74, 76, 84, 106, 162, 170
as the Christ, TP: 150

as "the door" and "the way," P: 32
as the Father incarnate, TT: 43, 141, 142, 169
as the Messiah, ASP: 144, 166
as "the way," MJ: 102, 131
as the Word, CH: 61, 62; MG: 44
as transcendent soul, ASP: 24, 143
as type man, TM: 4, 40, 70
as type of new race, ASP: 33, 34, 168, 169
as Way-Shower, ASP: 152, 153, 154; KL: 41, 57, 107,
    127, 128, 129, 162, 164, 185, 186, 197; P: 106;
    TM: 3, 4, 109, 114, 118, 119; TP: 64; TT: 141
as Word of God, KL: 20
ascension of, through body regeneration, JC: 72, 73, 83,
    84
at-one-ment of, MJ: 128, 129; TT: 161, 178 (atone-
    ment)
authority of, KL: 15, 29, 55, 72, 73
available to all, KL: 164
baptism of, TM: 89
belief in, MJ: 38
betrayal of, MJ: 116, 117, 128
birth of, interpreted, TP: 49, 123
blood of, (see *Jesus, body and blood of*)
body and blood of, ASP: 76, 77, 78, 169; JC: 144, 145,
    158, 159; KL: 27, 28, 133, 134, 166, 167
body of, ASP: 77, 122, 144-146, 149, 169; KL: 20,
    131-134; MJ: 15, 167, 171-173, 181; P: 78, 79;
    TM: 70, 119, 120, 135
    offered as life transformer, KL: 132-134
    resurrected, MJ: 15, 167, 171, 172, 173, 181 (see
        Jesus, resurrection of)
    vs. astral, ASP: 146, 147, 168, 169
born to be Way-Shower, KL: 197
born to save human family from extinction, JC: 4
brought forth the Christ, KL: 112
brought good news of salvation from death, KL: 20, 21,
    96, 160, 185
called Word of God, CH: 61, 62
calling on name of, (see *Jesus, using name of*)
came to give life, KL: 132
came to mend spiritual law, TM: 44

152

formed spiritual zone on earth, JC: 83, 87, 110
formulas of, KL: 41, 42
freedom in declaring and decreeing words of, ASP: 54,
    55, 82
gave blood transfusion to race, KL: 132, 133, 134, 166
gave credit to Father for great works, JC: 17, 141;
    KL: 51, 55; TP: 102
glorification of, MJ: 147-151
glorifying God in one's body according to, ASP: 80
Gospel of John as a symbolical life of, MJ: 12
greatness of, JC: 110; TT: 67; KL: 128, 129
had prosperity consciousness, P: 90, 91, 166, 186, 187
healed sick and raised dead, KL: 173
healing method of, JC: 3-5, 41, 45, 56, 57, 58, 94, 95,
    96, 103 (see *Jesus, and healing*)
higher law at work at death of, MG: 164
His advent planned and orderly, JC: 118, 119
His part in opening man's way to glory, MJ: 16, 88, 149,
    150
His relation to the Father, TT: 142, 143
His tribute to woman, MJ: 162
imagination and will as used by, P: 78, 79
importance of superman as thinking power realized by,
    ASP: 61
incarnation of, as pattern for man, MJ: 35, 36
instructions with respect to prayer, TP: 4, 16, 17, 81
inward happiness of, MG: 184
key to development of, KL: 50, 51
kingdom of, TM: 67, 68, 69
knowledge and power of, CH: 98
lack of scholastic advantages of, ASP: 89, 90
laid claim to prior existence, KL: 129, 130
lives today, KL: 187
man as, KL: 116
manifestation and, JC: 156, 158, 163
man's joint heirship with, ASP: 123; KL: 27
man's relation to, TT: 168, 169
mastered two currents in body, KL: 74
matter and, ASP: 9, 10; MJ: 126
mental science vs. teachings of, ASP: 56, 73
mind and body of, raised to His supermind level, JC: 13,

on oneness with Father, JC: 5, 50, 97, 99; KL: 18, 27, 29
on perfection of man, CH: 24
on personal appearing of the Christ, ASP: 171
on physical resurrection, KL: 21, 99
on relation of works to spiritual power, MJ: 105
on release and control of electronic energy, TM: 5
on resistance and antagonism, KL: 175
on single eye, KL: 21
on sin of poverty, P: 60-62
on spiritual faith, CH: 87-89, 91
on states of consciousness, TT: 84
on talking, KL: 74
on tension, TM: 160
on the greater works expected of man, ASP: 30, 70, 71, 58, 61
on the law of judgment, CH: 121, 122
on understanding of faith, P: 42
on unity of all men, CH: 25
on what He expects of His followers, TP: 77, 102
on will and understanding, CH: 107, 108
on zeal, TP: 128
opened way out of race thought into spiritual realm, KL: 185
original doctrine of, and His disciples, TT: 102-104
overcoming of, MG: 258
parables of, ASP: 59, 102; JC: 84; TM: 34; TP: 15; TT: 155, 158
part played by intellectual and pseudo-spiritual forces in crucifixion of, MJ: 113, 114, 161, 162
passion of, KL: 138
personality of, merged in Universal, CH: 15, 27; KL: 194, 195 (see *personality, Jesus and*)
Peter's recognition of Christ in, CH: 67
power of, MJ: 80, 173
praise of, KL: 189
prayer, of, KL: 65, 72
prayers of, as positive affirmations, P: 112-113
promises of, should be taken literally, ASP: 82; P: 36, 37

promulgated laws for His kingdom, TM: 67, 68

prosperity consciousness of, P: 90, 91, 166, 186, 187

purified body of, as seed in race consciousness, TM: 158

raised up whole man, KL: 197

redemptive work of, KL: 26, 27, 127, 128, 166, 167, 168, 169, 185

refers to Holy Spirit as Comforter, KL: 16

regenerative work of Christ through, TM: 119-120

relationship of, to human family, KL: 129

release of electronic energy and its control as taught by, TM: 5

represents man in regeneration, KL: 163

response of, to united prayer, JC: 12, 155

Resurrection of, ASP: 11; KL: 13, 162; MJ: 167, 171, 172, 173, 175, 180, 181 (see *Jesus, body of, resurrected; resurrection*)

revealed in strong words, JC: 94, 95

sacrifice of, MJ: 123-125

salvation through, JC: 132, 162, 165

saves from sin, (see *sin, Jesus saves from*)

sayings of, ASP: 9, 10, 11, 12, 14, 18, 24, 30, 32, 37, 38, 41, 57, 59, 71, 82, 95, 96, 100, 101, 122, 129, 149, 162, 171; CH: 20, 24, 77; JC: 77, 132, 133, 149, 154, 158, 164; KL: 16, 17, 34, 51, 52, 55, 74, 88, 102, 107, 108, 114, 124, 161; MJ: 76, 89; P: 36, 37, 38, 47, 88, 112, 134, 135, 156, 157, 175; TM: 48, 62, 63, 65, 67, 68, 69, 72, 92, 105, 106, 109, 112, 116, 134, 135, 138, 172, 173; TP: 22, 30, 31, 58, 60, 65, 77, 78, 84, 87, 102, 110, 111, 113, 116, 119, 122, 123, 130, 153, 157; TT: 25, 75, 166, 175, 176

second coming of, ASP: 169; KL: 26; JC: 12, 20, 149, 150

service exemplified by, MJ: 126, 127

set precedent for Lent, KL: 3

showed that God's Will for man is health, ASP: 76

symbology of body and blood of, ASP: 77, 78

symbology of lowly birth, TP: 26, 49

taking literally promises of, ASP: 82

taught and proved immortality of body, ASP: 131, 169 (see *immortality*)

taught freedom from mortality, ASP: 82, 142, 143, 144, 145, 150, 151, 152, 169

words of, JC: 88, 89, 90
   to be kept by men, JC: 98, 99; TM: 61
   worked with law, JC: 129

Jetheth, MG: 291

Jethro, JC: 164

Jetur, MG: 207

Jeush, MG: 277, 278

Jew(s), KL: 32, 104; MG: 151; MJ: 41, 47, 48, 49, 59,
   60, 65, 77, 78, 88, 89, 91, 98, 102, 103, 114, 156,
   157, 158, 161, 164; TM: 113, 114; TP: 165 (see
   Israelites)

jewels, of gold, TM: 127
   of silver, TM: 127

Jidlaph, MG: 186

Joan of Arc, TP: 117

Job, ASP: 163; CH: 102, 103; JC: 53, 83, 164; MG: 37;
   P: 14, 19, 170; TP: 4, 6, 77-79, 85, 117, 129, 130
   (see *dreams*)

Jobab, son of Joktan, MG: 107
   son of Zerah, MG: 289

John, the apostle, ASP: 22, 44, 163; JC: 164; MG: 16;
   MJ: 167; TM: 20, 81; TP: 102, 166; TT: 66 (see
   love)
   and Book of Revelation (1st chapter) explained, TP: 61,
   62
   and his vision of Jesus, ASP: 83; KL: 187; TM: 7, 8
   and love, ASP: 152, 153; CH: 73, 92; MJ: 20, 155,
   162, 180
   and Revelation, chapter 1, explained, JC: 190; TP: 61,
   62, 63
   as symbol of love faculty, ASP: 40, 152; CH: 73, 92,

161

132, 133; KL: 34, 117; MG: 237; MJ: 20, 155, 162;
P: 45; TM: 16, 20, 45, 133; TT: 53
Jesus Christ and, CH: 132; MJ: 12
on New Jerusalem, ASP: 163; TT: 128, 129, 159, 160
parallel between Genesis and, MJ: 12 (Spirit), MG: 236,
237

John the Baptist, and Jesus, ASP: 122, MJ: 12, 17; P: 44,
45; TM: 89, 90, 91, 151, 152, 157; TP: 67, 68
and personality, TP: 67, 68
and receptivity, TM: 156
and renunciation, JC: 62; KL: 141; TM: 32, 151-157;
TP: 67, 68
as illumined natural man, MJ: 13, 18, 19
as intellectual perception of Truth, MJ: 14, 41, 42;
P: 44, 45; TM: 88, 153; TT: 69
as reincarnation of Elijah, TP: 72
vs. Son of God, JC: 61, 62

John, the Gospel of, KL: 98; MG: 16, MJ: entire book;
TM: 7; TP: 60, 61, 62; 66, 123, 166
on mystery of Jesus, JC: 190; KL: 130; TM: 7;
TP: 60, 61, 62, 119
on New Jerusalem, TT: 128, 129, 159, 160

Jokshan, MG: 202

Joktan, MG: 105, 108

Jonahs, TP: 106

Jordan, MG: 124, 126, 257; MJ: 105; TP: 148-153

Joseph, husband of Mary, ASP: 143, 144; CH: 103;
P: 44; TT: 137
of Arimathea, KL: 195, 196; MJ: 165
son of Jacob, ASP: 20; MG: 261, 262, 293, 362, 376;
MJ: 44; TM: 102, 121 (see *dreams; imagination*)
and death, MG: 371, 376
and dreams, MG: 293, 294; TM: 72, 81, 97, 98;

TM: 16, 22, 23
as representing selfishness, MJ: 116, 117; TM: 22
as sense consciousness, CH: 58, 59, 74; MJ: 116, 117
consciousness, (see *consciousness, Judas*)
false ego; false state of consciousness, CH: 58, 59
representative of generative life, TM: 161-174
was a thief, CH: 58

Judea, MJ: 41, 46, 47, 77 (see *Judah*)

judge, ASP: 45, 46

Judge, the Son as supreme, CH: 126

judgment, ASP: 75, 76; KL: 75, 161; MG: 23, 99, 146,
    257, 373, 375; MJ: 64 (see *discrimination; zeal;
    death; judgment day and; Jesus, and judgment; justice*)
  and affirmation, ASP: 45-47; CH: 125, 126
  and criticism, MJ: 65; P: 118
  and justice, CH: 119-128
  and Principle, CH: 121
  and regeneration, TM: 133
  and wisdom, TM: 41-51
  and zeal, TP: 126, 127
  as a faculty, TT: 53, 54
  as represented by James, son of Zebedee, ASP: 40, 152;
    CH: 92; P: 45; TM: 16, 19, 20, 41-51, 133
  as vengeance, MG: 266, 269
  carnal, TT: 87
  day of, ASP: 155; TM: 43, 44
  discrimination, MG: 23, 146, 185, 199, 299
  divine, KL: 182, 183; MJ: 76
  good, and Principle, CH: 121, 122
  I AM and, CH: 29, 121, 122
  mortal, KL: 182; MJ: 65, 86
  of spiritual things, ASP: 123
  passing, by affirmation and denial, ASP: 45-47
  personal, CH: 122, 124, 125
  relation of thought creations to, ASP: 48, 49; P: 125
  represented by Dan, MG: 135, 238, 275
  represented by Kemuel, MG: 186

K

kidney trouble, CH: 54

Kidron, MJ: 152

kill, ASP: 46

kindness, TP: 110, 113

King Lear, ASP: 113 (Shakespeare)

king(s), ASP: 19, 46, 47; MG: 133, 137, 317; MJ: 161,
    162; P: 77, 155, 182
  of Sodom, MG: 137

kingdom, indwelling spiritual, ASP: 149, 169
  of Christ, JC: 62
  of God, of heaven, (see *heaven; kingdom of the heavens;
    superconscious mind; supermind*)
    and prosperity, P: 88, 141
    and transformed body, TP: 15, 68
    as demonstrated by Jesus, P: 5, 6, 11, 12, 80, 81,
      166, 167, 186
    as divine order, JC: 130
    as fourth dimension, ASP: 56-62
    as realm of mind, ASP: 58; JC: 21, 47, 48, 83, 84,
      143
    as realm of superconscious mind in man, P: 33, 176
    attainment of, through thought, KL: 141, 142;
      TP: 68, 163
    can be set up in earth by right thinking, ASP: 16, 67,
      71; JC: 115, 189, 190; TT: 16, 32, 123-131
    Carlyle on, TP: 25 (see *mind*)
    how developed within man, KL: 30
    how established on earth, JC: 21
    how to enter, JC: 61, 62, 147, 189, 190; KL: 30,
      117, 167; P: 15, 16, 81, 82, 153; TM: 18, 68;
      TP: 27, 68; TT: 28-37, 142, 157
    I am and, TT: 28-37, 125
    keys to, KL: 117
    laws promulgated by Jesus for His, TM: 67-68
    location of, ASP: 9, 25, 58; JC: 71, 77, 115, 125;

167

Kings, TP: 148

Kiriath-arba (or Hebron), MG: 127, 189, 190, 192, 276

knowing, CH: 44, 55, 89, 98, 112, 114; JC: 32, 48;
    KL: 113, 114, 158; TM: 43, 47, 49, 85, 88, 90 (see
    intuition)

knowledge, ASP: 9, 20, 89; CH: 98; JC: 42; MG: 50,
    240; TM: 46, 84, 144; TP: 152; TT: 76, 114 (see
    wisdom; understanding)
  of Jesus, CH: 98
  tree of, (see *tree, of knowledge of good and evil*)

Koch, Robert, TM: 147-148; TT: 17

Kohath, MG: 345

Korah, MG: 277, 289

Krishna, CH: 23

L

Laban, MG: 199, 208, 225, 226, 233, 242-245, 247, 252, 253

labor, ASP: 16, 172; KL: 106, 107; P: 34, 186 (see *work*)

lack, (see *debt; poverty; need; understanding, lack of*)
  and mind, (see *mind, lack and*)
  cause of, KL: 101-103, 106; P: 19, 20, 46, 48, 52, 60-62, 67, 80, 82, 96-99, 157, 159, 167-168, 171
  defined, P: 59
  denial of, P: 37, 38, 41, 69, 93, 114, 119, 120, 121, 122, 123, 151, 157, 170, 177, 178, 179
  fear of, and how to overcome it, KL: 105; P: 23, 38, 48, 52, 53, 65, 68, 74, 75, 81, 85, 92, 113, 122, 166, 168, 169, 173-187; TT: 95
  mind and, (see *mind, lack and*)
  no, in God's universe, JC: 134; P: 38, 52, 87, 93, 95, 170
  not God's will for us, P: 46, 113
  overcoming fear (thought) of, P: 52-53, 92-93, 165, 166, 173-187
  periods of, and their cause, P: 96-99, 167-168
  remedy for, KL: 106; P: 19, 20, 21, 38, 46, 48, 52, 54, 80, 81, 103, 111, 113, 121, 177

ladder, MG: 226

lamb, TM: 128

Lamb, JC: 151
  of God, KL: 124; MJ: 18-20; TM: 60, 164-165

Lamech, son of Methuselah, MG: 69, 70, 74, 75
  son of Methushael, MG: 62, 63

land, MG: 357

dry, MG: 18
  flowing with milk and honey, KL: 56
  of Canaan, P: 99

language, a new, ASP: 22
  and mind, ASP: 88; JC: 34
  of God, JC: 33
  of the soul, JC: 33

lantern, MJ: 152

larynx, CH: 63, 64; KL: 74, 75; MJ: 24, 25, 27

Lasha, MG: 102

"last day", MJ: 75

last enemy, TM: 23

Last Supper, JC: 144, 145, 158, 159; KL: 133, 139, 192

laughter, JC: 168; MG: 145; TP: 132

law, CH: 38; JC: 95; KL: 32
  active in all nature, CH: 137; JC: 84, 85; KL: 131
  adverse action of, MG: 285
  affirmation for establishing oneself in, KL: 159; P: 59,
    60
  all true action is governed by, KL: 131; P: 58; TM: 38
  and health, JC: 3, 44, 53, 80, 117, 121, 159; MJ: 60
  and love, MJ: 129; P: 102, 110
  and understanding, CH: 55; JC: 42; P: 70
  applying divine, TP: 86-89
  as foundation of universe, JC: 129, 172; MJ: 36; P: 93
  as order, CH: 7
  as Truth, JC: 59, 60; KL: 160
  blind use of, MJ: 62, 137
  cannot be broken, KL: 131, 158
  Christ and God's, MJ: 11, 64, 65
  condemnation and, MJ: 66
  creative, JC: 5, 31, 67, 76, 172; P: 84; TP: 94;

173

race, (see *race law*)
recognition of Power of, KL: 32
represented by Moses, ASP: 156, 157
rules of, P: 59
scientific, P: 75
spiritual, ASP: 166, 167; CH: 37; JC: 3, 59, 84, 85,
    118, 119-124; MJ: 69; P: 66, 175, 176; TP: 30
    and order, TM: 110-129, 146
supreme, of God as Spirit manifesting in mind of man,
    ASP: 61
transgression of, ASP: 142; KL: 32, 161; MG: 46, 47,
    65, 75, 77, 138, 325, 326
unchangeable, P: 58, 59
universal, JC: 42, 44, 59, 72, 127, 129; KL: 47; P: 58,
    59, 68, 93; TM: 125, 126, 127, 129; TT: 111, 157,
    170
    works within man for reembodiment, KL: 93

lawmaking does not bring peace, TP: 107

laws, study of mental, CH: 12

lawsuits, TT: 86, 87

laxative, TM: 144

laying on of hands, ASP: 67

laying up for future, P: 152

Lazarus, ASP: 148; CH: 13; JC: 9, 39, 40, 78;
    MJ: 106-112, 115, 118
    brother of Martha and Mary, TT: 42, 47, 49
    parable of, and the rich man, P: 163
    raising of, MJ: 107-112
    the beggar, TT: 155-158

laziness, P: 111

lead, ASP: 51

leader, ASP: 59, 60, 167; JC: 156
  false, ASP: 128

leadership, MG: 127

leadings, MG: 139 (see *guidance, divine*)
  of the Spirit, ASP: 75

Leah, CH: 72, 74, 75, 76, 130; MG: 189, 233-237,
  239-242, 244, 261, 262, 274, 300

leaven, KL: 188, 196

Lebbaeus, (see *Thaddaeus*)

Leeser, Isaac, TT: 42

legislation, P: 26, 148

Lehabim, MG: 99

Leibnitz, Gottfried Wilhelm von, JC: 55

Lent, KL: 3-5, 138, 140, 166

leper, JC: 57, 75; TP: 148, 150, 151, 153

letter, P: 147

letting go, P: 142, 153, 174, 175, 176, 178

Letushim, MG: 203

Leummim, MG: 203

Levi, CH: 74, 75, 76, 130, 131; MG: 236, 237, 269, 275,
  344, 365, 366 (see *love; unity*)

levitation, CH: 27; MJ: 174, 175

liberty, statement for claiming, TP: 184

license, CH: 112, 113

life, ASP: 97; CH: 35, 36; JC: 134; KL: 59, 60, 61;
    MG: 46, 365; TM: 139; TP: 17, 98 (see *death;*
    Judas)
  affirmations for more, JC: 13, 14, 161, 173; KL: 149,
    165, 186; TT: 152 (see *affirmation, life and*)
  and sensation, CH: 47, 56, 58, 59
  and substance, MG: 22, 352; P: 13, 45, 46, 47, 51
  appropriation of, ASP: 157; KL: 58, 122, 123, 124,
    161; TP: 27, 28, 184, 185
  as abiding flame in man, KL: 162, 185, 186
  as an idea, CH: 44, 46; JC: 103, 104; P: 29, 156, 157;
    TT: 18, 42, 43, 44
  as energy, ASP: 12, 13; KL: 132, 133; MJ: 31;
    TM: 161; TP: 64, 65 (see *atomic, energy*)
  as gift of God, KL: 20, 161
  as Mind, JC: 105
  as omnipresent, KL: 122, 123
    and eternal, MG: 105
    and omnipotent, MJ: 63
  as principle and expression of Being, KL: 161; TT: 10,
    40, 41, 45, 46, 149
  as son of God, TM: 53
  as spiritual Being, TT: 154
  as universal energy, TP: 64
  attaining, of spirit, P: 179
  book of, (see *book of life*)
  center, in body, CH: 46, 47; KL: 123; MG: 217, 306;
    TM: 162, 163
  Christ, ASP: 24; JC: 158, 159; MJ: 31, 102, 167
  compared to battle, MG: 265
  consciousness, JC: 17, 64, 94, 103, 105; KL: 122, 123,
    163; MG: 61, 305; TM: 22, 158, 161, 164; TT: 148
  conservation of, KL: 48, 49, 163
  current, JC: 162, 169; KL: 73
    and right relation of ideas, JC: 4, 5, 104, 162, 163,
      169
    how changed, KL: 126
    how to make flow, KL: 74, 161
    subject to word of man, KL: 73, 74

176

defined, JC: 29; KL: 161
desire and, TM: 131
difference between essence and living, KL: 60
divine, KL: 122-126; MG: 22, 23, 24, 25, 69, 149 (see
  Methuselah; Lamech)
effect of thoughts and words on, CH: 46, 47; JC: 16,
  42, 104, 105, 133; KL: 73, 74; TP: 170
ego, TM: 161
error tendencies in subjective, MG: 284
eternal, TP: 21
  and mind, MJ: 110, 111
  as gift of God to man, MJ: 48
  attainment of, ASP: 13, 24, 30, 53, 54, 66, 101, 131,
    147, 148, 149, 150, 151, 176; KL: 55, 56, 57,
    95-99, 122-135; MJ: 47, 48, 58, 63, 69, 81, 93,
    110, 111, 147, 149, 168, 173, 181; TM: 23, 170;
    TT: 146-160, 176
  crown of, KL: 167
  hindrance to, KL: 122, 123; MJ: 154
  is for both body and soul, ASP: 13, 24, 30, 66, 131,
    142; KL: 68, 69, 70, 93, 94 (see *body, as poten-
    tially eternal*)
  Jesus and, ASP: 37; JC: 146, 147, 156, 157, 159;
    KL: 74, 93-100, 122, 124, 132, 162; MJ: 47, 48,
    63, 69, 74, 81, 109, 147, 149, 154, 168, 171, 172,
    173, 181; TM: 6, 7, 158, 170, 174; TP: 5, 14, 74;
    TT: 148, 149, 154
  Jesus Christ and, ASP: 44, 104; JC: 55, 56, 131, 132,
    133, 195; MJ: 169, 171; TP: 64, 65; TT: 148,
    155
  word and, JC: 105, 132, 133; TT: 146-160
faith and, MJ: 41, 110, 111; TP: 149, 150
Father as principle of, (see *Father, as principle of life*)
first step in realization of, KL: 123
forces, and faith, MG: 181
  and Judas, MJ: 128
  direction of, TT: 40
  must be lifted up, KL: 124, 125
fountainhead of, JC: 30, 98
fullness of, and life consciousness, JC: 104, 105
generative, TM: 161-174

lighting, JC: 150

likeness, (see *man, image-and-likeness*)

lilies, P: 34

limitation, MJ: 101
  desire to be free from, is universal, CH: 27
  false belief in, KL: 63
  God-Mind has no, TP: 15
  how to be made free from, ASP: 46, 101, 167, 169;
    KL: 63, 65, 197; MJ: 58, 89, 98, 100
  selfishness is, CH: 92
  thoughts of, KL: 13, 65, 106, 107, 197; MJ: 68, 76, 77,
    168; P: 52, 54, 55, 81, 82, 142, 162, 167, 175;
    TM: 111, 115; TP: 173

Lincoln, Abraham, ASP: 126

lion, P: 184; TM: 36

lip service, JC: 92

listening, TP: 117, 118

literature, metaphysical, ASP: 23

liver, CH: 24, 65, 99, 124, 125, 126 (see *condemnation*)
  statements for healing, TP: 181

living, TP: 22
  "God is not the God of the dead, but of the," ASP: 44
  riotous, P: 60, 61, 62
  "living bread," (see *bread*)
  making a, KL: 106

loaves and fishes, ASP: 10, 14, 102; CH: 64, 78, 80;
    JC: 145; MJ: 74; P: 19, 46, 79, 84, 100, 159 (see
    Jesus, and loaves and fishes)

locomotive, KL: 159

Lodge, Sir Oliver, TP: 53

logic, (see *reason*)
 argues against world's coming to an end, KL: 40
 as fundamental sense in man, CH: 8, 9
 human reason and, ASP: 19
 of being, CH: 10; JC: 190, 191
 of Truth, KL: 19

Logos, KL: 172, (see *Jesus, and Logos; Word of God*)
 and life, JC: 163; TP: 170
 and Word, CH: 61, 137; JC: 163; KL: 172; MJ: 76;
    TP: 167
 as creative Word or power of God, CH: 18, 61, 70, 137;
    JC: 15, 144, 161; MJ: 11, 93; MG: 17; TP: 17
 as idea containing all ideas, MJ: 11, 76
 as second in Trinity, KL: 15
 as the Father, TP: 168-174
 defined, CH: 18, 61; MJ: 11, 12; TP: 17, 66, 67,
    166-168, 172
 God as creative power, MJ: 11; MG: 16, 17
 in its healing aspect, TP: 164-174
 see also *Jesus; Word of God*

loins, TM: 16, 18

London Times, ASP: 114, 115

"Looking Backward" (Edward Bellamy), ASP: 31, 32

"loose him and let him go," MJ: 111, 112

loosing, P: 176, 177
 negative manifestations, KL: 118

Lord, P: 139, 164, 168, 180, 181, 184; TM: 121; TT: 45
    (see *Jehovah*)
 all men are chosen of, JC: 115, 116
 appeared to Saul, TM: 76
 as a mind in man, CH: 97; TP: 24
 as creative mind, P: 41

"loud voice," (see *voice*)

Lot, MG: 119, 122-126, 134, 164-170

Lotan, MG: 283, 284

Lot's wife, ASP: 71, 72; TM: 146; TP: 96, 98

love, P: 94 (see *Adah; female; heart; John; soul; woman*)
  and affirmation, MJ: 180
  and courage, CH: 138
  and debt, KL: 35; P: 118-124, 126
  and evil, MG: 299; TT: 56, 60
  and faith, ASP: 40; JC: 103; KL: 119, 120; MG: 126;
    MJ: 128, 179, 180
  and family, CH: 131
  and fear, MG: 257, 258; TP: 112-115
  and giving, P: 154, 155
  and gravity, TP: 108, 110
  and greed, TT: 54
  and hate, ASP: 148; P: 109, 118; TT: 152, 153
  and health, ASP: 104, 105, 149; MJ: 117; TP: 178
  and it's attributes, TT: 56, 61
  and judgment, CH: 121; MJ: 65
  and law, (see *law, and love*)
  and obedience, KL: 35
  and order, CH: 137
  and power, KL: 30, 31; TT: 58, 59
    of the word, CH: 65, 66, 136, 137, 138
  and prosperity, ASP: 35; P: 103, 108, 109, 150;
    TP: 34, 106, 107; TT: 60, 61
  and regeneration, CH: 131-139; KL: 151, 152;
    TM: 52-60, 133; TP: 110
  and sensation, TM: 43
  and sex lust, TT: 64
  and soul, CH: 130, 131; TM: 71
  and supply, ASP: 35; TP: 34; TT: 55, 61
  and understanding, CH: 139; KL: 31
  and will, KL: 30, 31
  and wisdom, KL: 31, 155; MG: 25, 27, 32, 33, 40, 41,
    42, 57; P: 29, 30; TM: 41, 49; TT: 58, 78, 79, 91,

183

127, 133, 134, 166
affirming of, KL: 34
as activated by thought, TT: 26, 29, 51, 51, 53
as a divine principle, TT: 52, 59
as binding factor, CH: 46, 130
as blind without wisdom, TT: 78, 79
as builder of mind substance, KL: 34
as daughter of God, TM: 53, 55
as divine ordinance, KL: 35
as essential to soul growth, P: 173; TP: 108, 109
as faculty of mind, CH: 81, 130; TM: 131
as fulfillment of law, MJ: 129, 135; P: 74, 110, 123,
    124, 139; TP: 113
as greatest commandment, P: 65
as great force, KL: 30, MJ: 117
as harmonizer, ASP: 72, 75; CH: 130-140; KL: 30;
    MJ: 139; TP: 107-111 (see *harmony, as affiliated
    with love*)
as idea of universal unity, KL: 151
as magnet, TT: 55, 56, 57, 60, 61, 153
    of supply, P: 103, 106, 108, 109, 110, 143, 144, 157,
        162; TT: 55, 61
as Principle, KL: 33
as regenerative power, TM: 53-60
as represented by Adah, MG: 63, 277
as represented by John, ASP: 40, 152; CH: 43, 132,
    133; KL: 34, 117; MG: 237; MJ: 20, 155, 162;
    P: 45; TM: 16, 20, 45, 133; TT: 53
as represented by Kohath, MG: 345
as servant, KL: 35; MJ: 115, 116
as solvent of debts, P: 122-124
as solvent of negative states, ASP: 72, 75; CH: 130,
    137, 138; KL: 30, 31; P: 73
as unifier, ASP: 44; CH: 73, 130-140; KL: 33;
    MG: 236, 237; P: 65, 151; TP: 109
balancing judgment with, MJ: 65
blunders made by, TM: 41; TT: 54
center in body, CH: 38, 130; KL: 34; P: 102; TM: 91;
    TT: 62, 63, 64
    affirmation for development of, TT: 63, 65
character development through, CH: 92, 93; KL: 152;

185

vs. sex lust, TT: 64
woman as representing, MG: 49, 50, 51; MJ: 162;
  TM: 59

Lowell, James Russell, JC: 191; TT: 122

lowland, MG: 153

loyalty, P: 65, 66

Lucifer, TM: 66

luck, CH: 87, 92, 93; P: 58

Lud, MG: 103, 271

Ludim, MG: 99

Luke, ASP: 101, 102

Luke, Gospel of, P: 43

lungs, MJ: 57, 58

lust, CH: 112, 113; JC: 58; KL: 59, 65, 123; MG: 129,
  280; P: 19; TM: 59, 146, 165, 167, 168, 169;
  TP: 154, 155, 181; TT: 20, 43, 50, 64, 144 (see
  passion; sex)

Luther, ASP: 129

Luther, Martin, JC: 71, 72, 85, 86
  and the Protestant Reformation, ASP: 129, 130

Luz (or Bethel), MG: 271, 359, 360

lying, JC: 179

M

Malchiel, MG: 348

Malchus, MJ: 153, 154

male, MG: 27 (see *man as male and female; wisdom*)

malice, TP: 178

mammon, P: 154, 155, 181, 185

Mamre, MG: 127, 135, 157, 192, 204, 276, 374

Man, (see *Son, of Man*)

man, KL: 54-62, 102; MJ: 107; TM: 124
  Adamic, CH: 55, 56; JC: 177, 178; KL: 60, 61;
    MG: 41, 67; TT: 14, 15 (see *Adam man*)
  adverse consciousness of, MJ: 158
  aligns self with law, KL: 158
  all mastery he attains is rooted in mind, ASP: 63, 148
  a molder—not a creator, ASP: 67, 93, 94; CH: 33
  and Christ consciousness, KL: 61, 98, 112; TT: 143,
    165, 166 (see *consciousness, Christ*)
  and Christ mind, TP: 138, 139 (see *mind, Christ*)
  and communion with God (see *communion, with God*)
  and conscience, (see *conscience*), KL: 44
  and debt, (see *debt*)
  and dominion, ASP: 41, 42, 45, 46, 52, 53, 61, 63, 71;
    CH: 51; TM: 113 (see *dominion*)
  and his lost contact with God, ASP: 68
  and his relation to God, KL: 29; P: 16, 40, 68, 70, 84,
    139, 162
  and his relation to other men, P: 16, 143
  and his spiritual unfoldment, TP: 11, 12, 13, 55-59, 68,
    69, 71, 73, 74, 75, 85, 88, 130 (see *man, evolution of;
    soul, development of man's; unfoldment*)
  and I AM, TT: 25 (see *I AM*)
  and ideas, ASP: 94-97; JC: 16, 18, 72, 120, 147, 166,
    176; KL: 110; P: 32, 95, 173; TM: 34, 35, 49;
    TP: 88; TT: 117, 118 (see *ideas, man, as idea in mind
    of God*)

and identification with Spirit, KL: 18, 58, 65
and imagination, CH: 96-106 (see *imagination*)
and intellect, TM: 71 (see *intellect*)
and justice, CH: 126 (see *justice*)
and law, KL: 60, 158; P: 59, 62, 63; TP: 177 (see *law*)
    of increase, P: 81 (see *increase, law of*)
and mind, ASP: 63, 87, 88, 117, 120, 141, 148;
    CH: 12, 13, 21, 22; KL: 116; MJ: 177
and power, JC: 194, 195; KL: 61, 119, 153; MJ: 130;
    P: 48, 181; TM: 61, 68, 133; TP: 88 (see *power*)
    of word, ASP: 149; P: 47
    through Jesus Christ, TP: 19, 59
    through thought, JC: 60, 71, 161, 162, 186
and prosperity, (see *prosperity; man, and supply*)
and psychic forces, TP: 48
and seven centers of his organism, TP: 154-156
and supply, (see *supply*)
and the Christ mind, TP: 138, 139
and the development of his twelve powers, TP: 58, 59
and understanding, (see *understanding*)
and unity with God, ASP: 68; CH: 36, 37, 63; KL: 53,
    84; JC: 27; MJ: 123; TP: 17, 88 (see *unity, with
    God*)
and words, CH: 64
animal, (see *man, physical; animal, nature of man*)
animal nature of, KL: 60
as a god, ASP: 129; CH: 25; JC: 158
as anointed son of God, TP: 79
as a son of God (God's idea), TT: 74, 90, 91, 103, 167,
    170
as born in Spirit, TT: 75-78, 80, 81 (see *man, spiritual-
    izing whole*)
as builder, (see *builder*)
as child of God, ASP: 58, 149; KL: 124, 143;
    MG: 103, 107, 292; P: 52, 182-185; TP: 4, 28, 87,
    88
as cocreator with God, ASP: 96, 99-102; CH: 68;
    JC: 143-145; KL: 54, 61, 110; MJ: 64; P: 91;
    TP: 17, 73, 77, 88, 94, 95, 98 (see *creation, is a
    cooperation between God and man*)
as cooperator with God in forming universe, CH: 33, 68;

189

JC: 143

as divine, ASP: 45, 46, 123

as dominant thinking and character-giving force, TM: 148, 149

as epitome of Being, CH: 42, 43; KL: 54, 55; MG: 75, 76

as eyes, ears, and mouth of God, ASP: 58

as focal point in God's consciousness, P: 29

as focus of Spirit, TP: 169

as free agent, ASP: 18, 19, 78, 96; CH: 109; KL: 29, 114, 119; MG: 76, 77; MJ: 140; TP: 101, 105, 124

as gardener, ASP: 141

as God in the making, TP: 49, 77, 78

as God-intoxicated, ASP: 59

as God sees him, KL: 15

as God's highest avenue of expression, CH: 68; TM: 35; TP: 20; TT: 41

as God's image and likeness, JC: 14, 15, 46, 47, 60, 74

as God's offspring, MJ: 46, 47

as God's supreme creation, JC: 9, 22

as heir to God's universal resources, CH: 36; KL: 142, 144; MJ: 38, 39; P: 16, 23, 52, 79, 90, 91, 98, 186

as idea in mind of God, CH: 20, 21, 22, 23, 24, 25, 33, 36, 37, 61, 62, 107; JC: 109; KL: 53; MJ: 145; TP: 20, 67, 160, 161; TT: 116-121, 161, 163 (see *Christ; man, and ideas; idea, man as one of God's*)

as image and likeness of God, ASP: 18, 53, 93, 98, 117, 122, 130, 135; CH: 19, 25, 26, 32, 33, 98, 108, 109; JC: 14, 15, 46, 47, 60, 61, 74, 127, 154, 191; KL: 17, 49, 59, 60; MG: 12, 24-26, 30, 33, 65, 75, 76, 231, 232, 347; P: 160; TM: 71; TP: 55, 77 (see *image and likeness*)

as imperishable Spirit, TM: 6, 130

as inlet and outlet of Divine Mind, P: 56-69

as inlet and outlet of life, substance, and intelligence, ASP: 94-97, 135-141; CH: 22, 23; JC: 25, 26

as Jesus, KL: 116

as key to Bible, JC: 71

as key to God and universe, CH: 19, 32, 42

as king, ASP: 19, 47

as light-center, TP: 61

as light of God, ASP: 58
as like his Parent, CH: 8, 20; P: 42
as male and female, TM: 35, 58, 59, 100, 166; TP: 130
as Mind, KL: 116
as mouthpiece of God, CH: 33
as organizer by nature, TT: 105
as outpicturing of creative Mind, ASP: 58
as planned by God, TP: 55
as power of God in action, KL: 153; TM: 68
as representing wisdom, MG: 40, 41, 50, 52; P: 29, 30
as responsible for others, MJ: 123
as responsible for bringing forth perfection, TT: 117,
    118
as ruling power in universe, MJ: 130
as seed of word of God, ASP: 59, 135, 136, 137, 138
as Son of God, ASP: 42; JC: 18, 101; MJ: 17, 18, 42,
    43, 162
as son of God, ASP: 36, 37, 46, 149; MJ: 47, 163;
    TP: 84; TT: 74, 143, 144, 163, 167
as spirit, ASP: 28
as spirit, soul, and body, CH: 72; JC: 71, 72;
    MG: 10-12, 99, 231, 307; MJ: 32, 149, 181;
    TM: 138; TT: 157-159
as steward of God, P: 152, 153
as supreme creation of God, JC: 9, 10, 15, 22, 127;
    P: 64, 160
as symbolically described in Bible, CH: 72-76; TP: 140
as temple of God, CH: 11, 12; JC: 24, 115, 116, 174,
    175, 185
as threefold being, MG: 10-12
as transformer of all things, KL: 55
as undefinable as God, KL: 56
as will of God, CH: 108, 111
    made manifest, KL: 61, 62, 110, 157, 167
Bible as allegorical record of, (see *Bible, as allegorical
    record*)
body of, (see *body*)
"born blind", MJ: 96, 97
brotherhood of, P: 136, 143 (see *brotherhood*)
brought forth by orderly process, JC: 118
can appropriate ideas of Divine Mind, P: 9, 29

future, ASP: 53, 68, 85; MJ: 37
in spirit, soul, and body, ASP: 31-44, 59, 60, 64,
68-71, 74, 99-105, 130, 138-141, 150-159,
163-172; CH: 26, 27, 32-37, 42, 43, 56-59, 93,
101, 102, 116, 117; JC: 10, 11, 144, 147, 178;
KL: 49, 54-62, 69, 79-82, 93, 97, 98, 127,
140-147, 158, 161, 162, 165, 166, 188-190, 193;
MG: 65, 67, 68, 106, 140, 210, 223, 301, 307,
371; MJ: 25-29, 35-38, 41, 43, 66, 70, 87, 92, 93,
109-112, 124, 139, 152, 162, 163, 182; P: 18, 27,
39, 64, 65, 76, 109, 156, 173, 176; TM: 3, 4, 15,
35, 37, 38, 39, 40, 54, 55, 61, 70, 79, 80, 89,
100-104, 114, 120-129, 135, 146, 150-156, 173,
176; TP: 17, 18, 40, 43, 44, 48, 50, 52, 56-69, 71,
74, 75, 84, 85, 88, 108-110, 140-147; TT: 35, 89,
90, 122-124, 139, 161-178 (see *evolution; regeneration*)
race, KL: 127, 130, 131, 134
social, KL: 32
statements of Truth to expedite, JC: 37, 38;
KL: 188, 190
faculties, or powers, of, JC: 152; KL: 110-121; P: 77;
TM: 49, 62; TP: 55-59 (see *faculties of man, twelve*)
faith and, ASP: 40; JC: 100, 101; MJ: 37 (see *faith*)
fall of, ASP: 68, 95, 136, 137; CH: 34, 47, 56; KL: 54,
60, 115, 130, 131, 132, 133; MG: 43, 44, 54, 55,
115, 278; MJ: 36, 37; TM: 57, 104; TT: 30, 31, 45,
108, 147, 161, 162, 163
Father principle in, MJ: 131, 132
fellowship between God and, MG: 277
flesh, JC: 62; TM: 6 (see *flesh, man*)
foolish beliefs about God, KL: 44
forms but does not create, ASP: 93
generic, CH: 55 (see *Adam*)
gives way to Christ man, KL: 95
goal of, ASP: 26, 123; KL: 93; P: 11; TT: 159
God's ideal conception of His perfect, JC: 16, 39, 109,
114; KL: 15
great privileges of, KL: 58
happiness as natural to, TP: 133, 173, 174
has authority over ideas of Infinite Mind, JC: 148; P: 9,

29 (see *dominion*)

has capacity for knowing and communing with God, JC: 24

has capacity to reform world about him, KL: 38

has glorious inheritance, TM: 64

has God capacity, ASP: 41, 42, 58, 71; JC: 71, 145

has inherent desire to excel, JC: 100

has lost contact with God, ASP: 68, 95 (see *man, fall of*)

has power to form and make manifest, CH: 62, 63, 68, 69; JC: 145, 176; P: 59; TM: 71; TT: 15, 70, 71 (see *man, power of; man, powers of*)

health is God's will for, ASP: 76

health is his birthright, JC: 23 (see *health*)

his prerogative to blot out error, TT: 25

history of, ASP: 68, 70, 116

Holy Spirit and, ASP: 38, 39, 99; TT: 138, 141

Holy Spirit revealed to, through his spiritual nature, TT: 139, 140

I AM, KL: 84

idea, (see *Christ man*)

ideal, KL: 110

    vs. intellectual, MG: 26

impeded by ignorance of his place in Being, KL: 55, 56, 57

imperfection in, KL: 59

importance of, in scheme of life, ASP: 52, 60, 61, 62, 63, 96

inability of, to receive fullness of power, JC: 194, 195

in midst of a race transition, ASP: 70, 71

intellectual, CH: 101; KL: 79, 81; MG: 26, 131, 210, 223; MJ: 131; TP: 139-147

    vs. spiritual, TT: 72

interspersed with Christ mind in God, ASP: 62

inventions of, duplicated in bodily activity, TM: 135, 136

inventive genius of, ASP: 52

is *I*, KL: 58

is never separated from God, JC: 36

is starting point of every thought and act, CH: 42

is to make manifest the works of God, MJ: 97

I will, TP: 17

same creative process used by God and, MJ: 11

seed of, MG: 51

self-knowledge revealed by I AM in, TT: 76

sense, CH: 56, 57, 58, 59, 75; KL: 60, 61; MG: 106, 130, 137, 207, 301; P: 97; TP: 139-147; TT: 129, 157

set free by Jesus Christ righteousness, JC: 61

sevenfold and twelvefold nature of, MJ: 68, 69

should be truly alive, KL: 185, 186

should have compassion of all life, KL: 122, 123

should talk to God about problems, KL: 20

significance of, ASP: 42, 43

smooth, MG: 220, 221

Son of (see man, Jesus Christ; Son, of man)

son of (see son, of man)

Son-of-God consciousness in, TM: 44, 45, 47

soul and body as helpmeets to, MG: 40 (see soul)

soul of, contains all attributes of infinite Mind, P: 76 (see soul)

spiritual, ASP: 13, 14, 34, 45, 57, 68, 103, 157, 165; CH: 27; JC: 9, 10, 35, 62, 74, 101, 103, 157, 178; KL: 36, 38, 58, 66, 67, 190; MG: 4, 5, 10-12, 26, 29, 33, 38, 40, 41, 42, 43, 44, 62, 63, 68, 69, 263, 264, 271; MJ: 12, 13, 36, 37, 76, 131, 132, 135, 141, 162, 177; P: 97, 151, 155, 163-172; TM: 6, 7, 8, 54, 116, 155, 163, 167; TP: 29, 48, 49, 59, 140, 141, 161, 163, 164

abilities of, ASP: 13

Christ as, CH: 23, 107, 120 (see Christ man; Christ as spiritual)

I AM as, CH: 33, 34

inheritance of, CH: 36, 116

perfect Word of God as, CH: 61, 62

spiritualizing the whole, ASP: 44, 70-79, 153, 154 (see man, as born into Spirit)

strong, TM: 34, 35

subconscious substance and life in, MG: 103

superconsciousness as potential in every, ASP: 59, 60, 128 (see mind, superconscious)

supermind and, ASP: 64 (see mind, superconscious)

tendency of, to go to extremes, MG: 281

Medan, MG: 202

mediator, JC: 194, 195

medical profession, TP: 152

medicine, ASP: 43, 89; CH: 105; JC: 80, 129, 132, 170
  vs. metaphysics, TT: 18, 19, 20

mediocrity vs. greatness, JC: 147

meditation, ASP: 51; MG: 228; TP: 118 (see prayer)
  benefits resulting from regular, CH: 15, 86, 132;
    JC: 11, 125; KL: 5, 12, 15; MG: 254; MJ: 92;
    P: 44, 129, 174; TM: 108
  Christ body as built through, ASP: 78
  energy released through, TM: 5
  "inner chamber" and, JC: 77
  prayer and, ASP: 11, 81, 104; JC: 70; P: 44
  prosperity and, P: 33, 34, 35, 53, 54, 129, 174
  spiritual man and, ASP: 104
  thoughts for, P: 53, 54
    (see prayer)

mediums, TP: 50, 116, 117

mediumship, CH: 113; JC: 160; MJ: 101, 102; TM: 109,
    171, 173; TT: 36 (see hypnotism; mesmerism)

medulla oblongata, TM: 16, 22, 140, 141; TP: 127

meekness, KL: 50, 51; TM: 89, 122, 123, 154; TT: 60,
    64, 93, 113

Mehetabel, MG: 290, 291

Mehujael, MG: 62

Melanchthon, Philipp, JC: 71, 72, 85, 86

Melchizedek, MG: 136

melody, MG: 64

memory, KL: 89, 90, 98, 99; TM: 138

men, holy, P: 10
  young, MG: 184, 185
  and women, ASP: 31

mental, P: 146, 147
  affirmations, ASP: 50
  attitudes, ASP: 11
  conception, KL: 24
  domains, ASP: 19
  laws, (see *laws, mental*)
  picture, (see *picture, mental*)
  science, ASP: 73 (see *science, mental*)
  suicide, ASP: 46

mentality, ASP: 19

Merari, MG: 345

merchant, P: 156

"Merchant of Venice", ASP: 115

Mesha, MG: 107

Meshech, MG: 93

Mesmer, Franz, JC: 45, 46

mesmerism, TM: 109 (see *hypnotism*)

Mesopotamia, MG: 199

Messiah, ASP: 144, 166; CH: 23, 76; JC: 10; MJ: 17, 65;
  MG: 366, 367; TT: 16, 17 (see *Krishna*)

messiah, ASP: 160

Metaphysics, ASP: 23, 34, 106-115; JC: 100, 141, 172, 173; MJ: 11; P: 148; TP: 96; TT: 18, 20, 39, 67, 68, 70, 72, 130, 161 (see *treatment, metaphysical; science, and metaphysics*)

metaphysicians, ASP: 29, 50, 54, 60, 103, 104, 112, 115, 132, 144, 145; CH: 42, 43, 50, 51, 56, 57, 58, 66, 101, 110, 113, 120, 121, 124, 127, 136, 137; JC: 121, 122, 156, 182, 183, 187, 188; KL: 19, 38, 71, 77, 140; P: 10, 46, 72, 76, 128, 149, 154, 178; MG: 122; MJ: 157; TM: 27, 83, 84, 119, 124, 128, 129, 134, 143, 144, 145, 158, 163; TP: 18, 34, 43, 79, 83, 91, 97, 98, 100, 109, 121, 140, 158; TT: 18, 19, 20, 42, 44, 112, 116, 119, 120, 130, 152, 162 (see *treatment, metaphysical*)

metaphysical treatment (see *treatment, metaphysical*)

Methodist, TT: 109

Methuselah, MG: 69

Methushael, MG: 62

Me-zahab, MG: 290, 291

Mibsam, MG: 206

Mibzar, MG: 292

Michelangelo, ASP: 83; P: 94

Michtam, TP: 136

microbes, TT: 18-27

microorganisms and thought, TT: 14-27

microwaves, ASP: 64

Midian, JC: 164; MG: 202, 203

Midianites, ASP: 54; MG: 145, 146, 299

"Midsummer Night's Dream", ASP: 106

Milcah, MG: 114, 185, 199

milk and honey, KL: 56

Mill (John Stuart), MG: 83

millennium, ASP: 53; KL: 39; MG: 111; TM: 32;
    TT: 124, 125

Miller, Hugh, MG: 3

Millikan, Prof. Robert Andrews (quoted), ASP: 164, 165

Mind, JC: 40, 105, 130, 172; KL: 116; P: 33; TT: 70
    (see *creative Mind; kingdom of God; mind*)
  active and passive side of, MG: 126
  affirmation and denial as dual attributes of, CH: 51-55
  affirmation for manifestation of, CH: 38
  and ideas, CH: 16, 18
  and prayer, TP: 177
  and spirit, as synonymous, CH: 11, 12
  as absolute and unlimited, CH: 66
  as everywhere present, CH: 66; JC: 118, 140; TP: 160,
    161
  as Father, MJ: 73; TP: 81, 82
  as generator of energy, TM: 32
  as generator of thought, TT: 8
  as integral substance, TP: 12
  as light, TP: 119, 120, 121
  as member of Trinity, JC: 122
  as reservoir of universe, ASP: 91, 93; CH: 14, 61;
    JC: 28, 100, 101, 127
  as source of all good, ASP: 90, 91
  as underlying cause, ASP: 92, 93; CH: 12; JC: 18, 45,
    100, 118, 126, 184, 191; TT: 16
  called into action by man's mind, P: 57, 60
  Christ, KL: 71, 77; MG: 58, 123, 127, 308; P: 75;

208

carried in the, CH: 34; KL: 20
controlled by, ASP: 20, 119; MG: 262
bound by time, space, and conditions, KL: 170
brain and, ASP: 34
can be trained to work systematically and reliably, KL: 89, 90
carnal, ASP: 148; KL: 194, 195; TM: 66; TT: 155
change of, changes things, ASP: 104, 105; TM: 32, 142, 143, 144, 145, 166
Christ, ASP: 56, 100; CH: 27, 28, 98, 115, 117, 120, 121; JC: 11, 52, 130, 131, 147, 150, 153; KL: 110-121, 172, 173, 193; MJ: 19, 20, 113; P: 74; TM: 119, 139, 140, 170; TP: 85, 138; TT: 155, 158 (see *Mind, Christ; Christ, as spiritual mind*)
affirmations for attaining, TT: 138, 139
Christianity as science based on, CH: 43; JC: 143, 144
cleansing of, CH: 57, 58; KL: 3, 193, 194; MJ: 17
through denial, CH: 57, 58; KL: 4, 63, 195; MJ: 17, 98; P: 175
through forgiveness, P: 119
clouded, ASP: 81
communes with Mind, ASP: 89, 90, 91, 92, 93
concentration of, P: 41, 80, 84; TP: 130, 131 (see *concentration*)
condition as image in, ASP: 47, 104, 105
conscious, ASP: 52, 148; CH: 63, 96, 97; JC: 112; MG: 40, 51, 52, 121, 122; P: 66, 176; TM: 3
and cellular life, ASP: 147
and subconscious mind, KL: 87-92; MG: 189-192, 204, 308
as director of subconscious mind, ASP: 76, 77
control of consciousness in, KL: 77
faith in relation to, MG: 17, 116
off guard during sleep, ASP: 109
constituents of, CH: 62
construction as attitude of, CH: 51
continuity of, after death, TM: 173, 174
creations of, are ideas, ASP: 93
creative, MG: 325; P: 41, 49
as the Father, JC: 18, 47

211

155, 156

mortal, TM: 103, 104; TP: 50; TT: 48, 106

must be illumined by Christ, TP: 61

must ideate body as God substance, MG: 262

nature of, JC: 176; TT: 33

necessity for unity between mind of man and Divine
Mind, ASP: 43

negative state of, TM: 128

nerves and, JC: 168; P: 156

not subject to lack, KL: 64

of Being, TM: 52

of Christ, (see *mind, Christ*)

of Father, MJ: 180, 181

of flesh, KL: 78, 131

of God, CH: 21; JC: 179, 180; KL: 98; TP: 67, 124

of Jesus, (see *Jesus, mind and body of*)

of man is built on Truth, ASP: 39, 40, 57

is one important study of man, CH: 32, 42; KL: 38

of nature as man's servant, JC: 188

of Spirit, JC: 176; MG: 116; P: 174; TM: 36; TP: 15,
138, 139

off guard during sleep, ASP: 109

one, is all there is, CH: 97, 107; TP: 138

overloading the, TM: 144

Paul on, (see *Paul, emphasized importance of*)

peace of, JC: 176

perfection in, to be expressed by man, TT: 117-120

perfect-man body and creative, ASP: 120, 121

personal, CH: 55, 56; JC: 46

power of, over energy, TM: 63

over matter, ASP: 29, 30, 51; JC: 186, 187; KL: 66

spiritualized, ASP: 29, 30, 31, 49, 68, 69, 81

to attract one's own, P: 79

to bless or curse, TP: 141, 142

to build or destroy human body, CH: 52-54, 105;
JC: 128, 129

powers, or faculties, of, (see *mind, faculties of*)

prayer and, JC: 68; TP: 19

race, ASP: 29; TP: 141

radiates energy and receives in kind, KL: 38, 39, 80;
TP: 142

213

215

mist, MG: 33

mistakes, CH: 110

Mizpah, MG: 252

Mizraim, MG: 96

Mizzah, MG: 281

Moab, grandson, of Lot, MG: 170

Moabites, MG: 170

mole, healing of, JC: 127

molecules, CH: 44, 50, 137; JC: 41; KL: 132; TP: 60
    (see *atom*)

money, MG: 357 (see *wealth*)
  and an idea, P: 16, 17, 30, 80, 186, 187
  and happiness, P: 162, 163
  asking for, P: 93, 94
  as representing substance, KL: 106; P: 20, 162, 165,
    177
  deference to, KL: 105
  dependence on God and not on, P: 73, 82, 83, 166
  effect of our words on, P: 103
  getting of, P: 73, 150, 151, 156, 160, 161
    destructive thoughts about, P: 148, 149
  giving and, P: 152, 153
  hoarding of, (see *hoarding*)
  how to think about, KL: 102-107; P: 20, 31, 32, 73,
    108, 109
  increased by blessing, P: 24, 47, 99, 100
  Jesus and, P: 113, 186, 187
  love of, CH: 135, 136; P: 89, 90, 109, 162, 168;
    TT: 54, 55, 57
    Paul on, P: 162
  manipulation of, by greed, P: 147
  man should not be slave to, ASP: 34, 35; P: 9, 80;

Mount Horeb, KL: 3

"Mount of Jehovah," TM: 27 (see *"upper room"*)

Mount of Olives, MG: 84

mount of Transfiguration, (see *Transfiguration, mount of*)

mourning, MG: 373

mouth, TM: 141

movement, KL: 38

Mozart, TM: 139

multitude, MJ: 73, 74, 78, 118, 121

Muppim, MG: 350

music, ASP: 16; JC: 49, 173; KL: 111, 178; MG: 64;
    TP: 44, 116, 117

mustard seed, JC: 75

mystery, JC: 6; MG: 116
  in religion, CH: 96 (see *religion*)
  of Godliness, ASP: 21, 22
  Paul on, of Christ, ASP: 13, 168; CH: 106; JC: 52;
    KL: 27; MG: 41, 115

"Mysterious Universe" (Jeans), ASP: 169, 170

mysticism, JC: 139, 141; TP: 153

mystics, ASP: 29; JC: 87, 92, 139, 164; MJ: 150

N

Naaman, JC: 75; MG: 64, 349; TP: 148-154

Nahath, MG: 280, 281

Nahor, MG: 113, 185, 186, 187, 199

naked, MG: 51, 88, 89; TM: 168

nakedness, KL: 54

name, P: 126
  calling upon the Christ, ASP: 30, 82; P: 97, 98 (see
    Christ, asking and receiving in name of)
  change of, MG: 151, 264
  Jehovah's, TP: 18
  of Jesus, JC: 156; P: 187; TM: 47; TP: 84, 85 (see
    Jesus, using name of)
  of Jesus Christ, (see *Jesus Christ, name of*)
  power in, JC: 154, 155, 156, 164, 165, 180, 181;
    MG: 65
  symbolical meaning in each Bible, CH: 72

naming things, MG: 40, 65; TP: 97; TT: 15, 16, 18, 21,
  24

Naomi, P: 65

Naphish, MG: 207

Naphtali, MG: 238, 275, 351, 369

Naphtuhim, MG: 100

napkin, MJ: 112

Napoleon, JC: 106; KL: 47

Nathanael, MJ: 21 (see *Bartholomew; imagination*)

nation, P: 156

nations, ASP: 161
  and peace, TP: 101, 107

nature, ASP: 29, 34, 51; CH: 12, 41, 42, 66; JC: 34;
    MJ: 174; P: 90; TP: 30, 48, 97, 109; TT: 61, 120
  animal, (see *animal, nature of man*)
  divine, in man, JC: 123
  duality of, JC: 187
  healing power of, JC: 18, 170, 182
  is moved by universal Spirit, ASP: 18, 19
  man was given dominion over, ASP: 61, 63

navel, TM: 16, 22 (see *James, son of Alphaeus*)

Nebaioth, MG: 205, 226

need, JC: 54, 81; P: 39

negation, ASP: 128, 154; CH: 54; JC: 62, 63, 129;
    KL: 141; P: 70, 71, 82, 98, 103, 112, 113, 124, 170,
    177; TP: 106, 180; TT: 82, 83, 126, 149 (see *news-papers*)
  belief in, ASP: 76, 119, 142; KL: 5, 48, 49, 66, 67;
    TT: 45
  to get rid of, ASP: 76, 82

negative, the, TM: 42

Nehemiah, KL: 37

neighbor, P: 74, 113

Neith, MG: 348

Nephilim, MG: 73, 74

nerves, CH: 40, 45, 47, 64, 65; JC: 168-170; MG: 35-37,

258, 259 (see *center, nerve; tree*)

nervousness, TP: 179

nervous prostration, JC: 176; TM: 108, 132, 159, 160

nervous system, ASP: 24; TM: 58; TP: 79

nervous tension, P: 168 (see *tension, nervous*)

net, MJ: 177

neutrons, ASP: 13

new birth, (see *birth, new*)

New Jerusalem, ASP: 166; JC: 84, 115; TT: 112, 125, 128, 129, 159

Newman, Cardinal, KL: 87

newspapers, JC: 119, 129

New Testament, ASP: 36, 116, 117; CH: 27, 28; JC: 10, 182, 183; KL: 3, 15, 26; P: 11; TP: 166; TT: 133, 135, 139, 159, 160

New Testament, as work on spiritual physiology, CH: 27, 28

Nicodemus, CH: 28; JC: 10, 85; MJ: 33-35, 37, 82; TM: 80; TP: 15

night, MG: 16, 20, 81 (see *darkness*)

Nimrod, MG: 97, 98

nine, TM: 99

Nineveh, city, MG: 98, 99

Nirvana, MJ: 151

no, CH: 51

Noah, MG: 69, 70, 74-84, 87-90, 108, 109
   drunkenness of, MG: 88, 89
   symbolism of, MG: 69, 70, 80, 82

Nod, MG: 61, 62

noise, TT: 8

nomads, TM: 24, 25

nonresistance, CH: 135; KL: 30, 195; MG: 83 (see *dove*)

north, MG: 93

nose, ASP: 132; TM: 141

nostrils, MG: 34

numbers, significance of, MG: 11, 31, 81, 82, 181, 217,
   320, 321, 358, 359

O

oak, JC: 28; MG: 120, 152, 157, 192, 193, 271, 272, 292

oath, MG: 121, 194

Obadiah, MG: 221

Obal, MG: 107

obedience, KL: 189; P: 156; TP: 28; TT: 89-100, 113
  allegiance is shown by, KL: 169
  concerning spiritual, TT: 93-98
  divine guidance through, KL: 46, 150; TM: 116, 154, 155
  hard experiences avoided through, JC: 125; MG: 76, 77, 87; P: 59
  health through, JC: 53
  Jesus Christ inspired, TP: 57
  necessary for spiritual development, KL: 62, MG: 184; P: 19, 85; TM: 119, 156
  prosperity through, P: 138
  regeneration through, TT: 112, 113, 119
  salvation through, MG: 76, 77, 86, 87; MJ: 92, 135; P: 58, 59; TT: 113
  spirit of, KL: 35
  spiritual, ASP: 26-35, 73, 95, 96, 137, 138

objective, MG: 42

obligation, financial, P: 128

obstinacy, TM: 108

occult, the, CH: 21; JC: 19, 20

occultism, ASP: 60, 113, 163, 164; MG: 47

offerings, freewill, P: 134, 136 (see *freewill offerings*)

officers, MJ: 82, 153, 154

Ohad, MG: 344

Oholibamah, MG: 277

oil, MG: 258; P: 99, 100, 113; TP: 33, 34
    and meal, ASP: 10

old age, (see *age, old*)

old, letting go of, P: 174-176

"old man" vs. "new man", ASP: 124

Old Testament, KL: 15, 39; TP: 167; TT: 135

olive leaf, MG: 83

Omar, MG: 279

omnipotence, TP: 11

Omnipresence, CH: 66-68, 120, 121; JC: 36, 71, 90, 191;
    TM: 29, 116-118

omnipresence, ASP: 37, 157, 160; CH: 66-68; KL: 11,
    83, 122; MG: 229, 230, 244, 245; MJ: 46, 47, 131,
    132, 134; P: 164; TP: 11, 83, 84, 92, 120, 145;
    TT: 151 (see *immanence*)

omnipresent Intelligence, KL: 45

Omniscience, MJ: 146

omniscience, TP: 11; TT: 72, 151

On, MG: 319, 349

Onam, MG: 286

Onan, MG: 303, 345

oneness, KL: 152; MJ: 54; TM: 116, 117 (see *unity; Jesus, on oneness with Father; unity, with God*)
  with God, KL: 123, 167; TP: 83, 84, 87, 88, 145, 160, 161
    Jesus and, ASP: 37, 38, 103, 104; MJ: 173; TP: 93; TT: 169
    Jesus Christ and, ASP: 41; KL: 77, 78
  with All-Good, KL: 33
  with Christ Mind, KL: 77
  with Divine Mind, KL: 77
  with Father-Mind, KL: 113; TP: 177, 178
  with life, KL: 123
  with the Father, MJ: 133; TP: 109 (see *unity, with the Father; man's oneness with the*)
  with Spirit, KL: 11, 153; TP: 93

only begotten, CH: 62
  Son, CH: 16, 25; TM: 54, 118, 119

open-mindedness, MJ: 100

operations, TP: 104, 105

Ophir, MG: 107

opportunity, P: 94, 98, 165

optimism, P: 112, 113; TP: 108

optimist, ASP: 52

order, TM: 42, 110-129
  and thought, JC: 121
  as kingdom of heaven, JC: 130
  as law, CH: 7
  divine, CH: 37; JC: 112, 117-121, 129-131
  health and, JC: 117, 118

P

230

partnership with God, TT: 146, 147

passion, CH: 115; JC: 130, 176; KL: 50, 123; P: 19, 20,
  82; TM: 69, 155, 156
  of Jesus, KL: 138

Passion Sunday, KL: 138

Passover, MJ: 28, 114
  feast of the, TM: 128

past, body renewal and denial of, ASP: 156, 157
  do not look back at, ASP: 71, 72

Pasteur, Louis, TM: 147, 148; TT: 17

Pathrusim, MG: 100

patience, KL: 181, 182; P: 112; TP: 110, 113, 114
  affirmation for, KL: 182

patient, JC: 56; TP: 183

Patmos, island of, ASP: 83

pattern, ASP: 47; CH: 100, 101; TP: 24 (see *Moses; Jesus
  Christ as our pattern*)

Paul, ASP: 171; CH: 11, 36; JC: 29, 148; MG: 149, 151,
  199, 220; P: 21, 146, 164; TM: 63, 64, 66, 92, 93,
  115; TP: 51, 71, 161-163; TT: 50, 85, 86, 137 (see
  Saul)
  and Lord's body, KL: 19, TP: 50; TT: 117
  and reincarnation, ASP: 28, 120; JC: 13
  and Silas, JC: 75; TP: 82
  as Pharisee, ASP: 26
  as Zealot, ASP: 26, 27
  awakening of, TM: 92, 93
  conversion of, ASP: 26-29; JC: 12
  emphasized importance of mind, ASP: 15, 29; JC: 142;
    MG: 56, 260; MJ: 31, 182; P: 148; TM: 23;

visions of, CH: 102, 103

paupers, P: 155

Payne, John Howard, TM: 56

peace, ASP: 104; KL: 25; JC: 21, 142, 169, 177;
MG: 105, 212, 213, 285; P: 123
conferences, ASP: 172
forgiveness and, P: 119
how to gain, ASP: 72; KL: 41, 42, 175, 176, 181;
JC: 21, 40, 81, 82, 123, 141, 142, 151, 152, 169,
176; MJ: 37, 171; P: 97, 107; TM: 68; TP: 43, 44,
72
in nations and in world, ASP: 16; TP: 101, 107;
TT: 122-124
Isaac as representing, MG: 216
Ishvah as representing, MG: 348
Jerusalem as city of, MJ: 56, 114
Noah as representing, MG: 70
of Jesus Christ, JC: 21, 142; MJ: 171
of knowing God, KL: 9
of mind, JC: 176
our influence for, KL: 6
Paul on, KL: 6
prayer for, JC: 169; MG: 105; TP: 36, 37, 107
Prince of, (see *Prince of Peace*)
Shelah as representing, MG: 105
thought and, TP: 72, 101
Truth statements for realization of, JC: 122, 139, 176;
KL: 176; TP: 107
Zion as representing spiritual, TP: 134

Peleg, MG: 105

Peniel, or Penuel, MG: 260

Pentecost, JC: 76

Pentecostal baptism, JC: 194

people, ASP: 81; JC: 94 (see *thought, people*)

perception, P: 182-184
  faith and, P: 43, 44
  intellectual, MG: 41, 42, 50, 344; P: 44, 45
  material, ASP: 154
  necessity of death of material, ASP: 153, 154
  spiritual, CH: 9, 10; MG: 330; MJ: 26, 41, 50; TT: 97, 161, 162

perdition, son of, CH: 58

Perez, MG: 306, 307, 345

perfection, CH: 24; TT: 155
  attainment of Christ, CH: 23, 105, 106; JC: 49, 114; KL: 9-13, 18, 22, 23, 59, 166, 167; MJ: 97; TT: 119, 120
  divine idea of, KL: 12, 22, 23, 59, 166, 167; MJ: 97; TT: 119, 120 (see *Christ, as perfect God idea*)
  God as, KL: 144; TP: 172 (see *God, as perfect*)
  man an expression of God's, JC: 35
  of body, KL: 10, 11, 13, 19, 22, 167; TT: 93, 117, 118
  on bringing forth, CH: 105, 106
  Truth statements for realization of, CH: 17, 106; KL: 142, 144, 166, 167, 173, 186, 189, 192, 196; TP: 70

Perizzites, MG: 146, 269

persecution, MJ: 142, 154, 157, 161

perseverance, CH: 88

persistence, ASP: 32, 33, 75, 76, 126, 127; JC: 48, 68, 70, 85, 86, 175; KL: 139; P: 33, 34, 51, 65, 66, 71, 72, 75, 111, 112, 114; TM: 65; TP: 81

Personality, JC: 123; TM: 27 (see *individuality*)
  and inferiority complex, TP: 78, 79
  as means of development, TM: 99, 100

as representative of states of consciousness, MG: 293
denial as remedy for, CH: 53; MJ: 17
God and, JC: 34; KL: 53; TT: 134, 169 (see *God,
personality not an aspect of*)
Ishmael represents, MG: 155
Jesus and, CH: 15, 27; JC: 69, 157; KL: 194, 195;
MJ: 133, 134, 145, 153; TT: 167, 171 (see *Jesus,
personality of*)
Jesus Christ and, JC: 17
Job and, TP: 78
John the Baptist and, TP: 67, 68
king of Sodom represents, MG: 137
selfishness and, CH: 92

personal, the, ASP: 40, 41, 78, 79; CH: 58; JC: 62;
TT: 25, 93, 94

personal will, (see *will, personal*)

pessimist, ASP: 52

pestilence, P: 98, 137

pests, TM: 148

Peter, Simon, ASP: 156; JC: 83, 163, 166; P: 164, 176
(see *faith*)
and faith, CH: 73, 86, 91, 92; JC: 47, 106, 166
and healing, TP: 102
and love, (see *love, Peter and*)
and vision, (see *visions, of Peter*)
as aspect of I AM, TT: 16
as faith, ASP: 40, 152; JC: 47, 102, 103, 166;
KL: 114, 116-121; MJ: 13, 20, 21, 68, 126, 129,
153-155, 179, 180; P: 42, 45; TM: 16-18, 28;
TP: 102; TT: 52-54, 90, 102, 103
as illustration of faith's victory over doubt, CH: 91
as receptivity from above, TM: 134; TP: 118; TT: 90
as "rock", MJ: 13
as typifying man's immortal body, JC: 50
book of, TP: 24

calling of, TM: 17, 18, 45
Church and, CH: 86; JC: 50; TT: 102, 103
delivered from prison by angel, JC: 72
dreams and visions of, TM: 77-79; TT: 137
dreams of, (see *dreams, of Peter*)
failure of, MJ: 129
Jesus Christ and, CH: 86
on flesh-eating, TM: 78
on the Christ, the Son of God, CH: 66
visions of, TM: 78, 79; TT: 137

Peter the Hermit, ASP: 59

phallicism, MG: 194

Pharaoh, MG: 324, 354
  as representing ruling ego or will, MG: 122, 301, 318,
    340, 341, 355, 357; TM: 102, 125-129
  as representing sun, MG: 122, 308, 317
  as ruler of solar plexus, MG: 121, 122, 308, 317, 318,
    357
  Children of Israel and, TM: 122, 123, 128, 129
  dreams of, MG: 313, 321; TM: 72
  Moses and, TM: 122-125
  wife of, TM: 102

Pharisee(s), MJ: 142; TM: 157 (see *intellect*)
  as intellectualists, MJ: 60, 80, 81, 87, 97, 98, 112-114,
    121, 122, 152; TM: 151
  chief priests of the, MJ: 82, 83, 152
  Jesus and, ASP: 90, 100, 103, 145; CH: 23; MJ: 77,
    78, 80; TM: 110
  leaven of the, KL: 188
  Nicodemus as a, MJ: 33-35
  Paul as, ASP: 26

Pharpar (river of Damascus), TP: 149

phenomena, JC: 46; P: 27
  psychic, TP: 50-53

phenomenal, the, TM: 98, 124

Phicol, MG: 180, 216

Philip, JC: 190; MG: 239; MJ: 21, 25, 68, 119, 132; TM: 62 (see *power, Philip as representing*)

Philistines, MG: 100, 102, 180, 214, 215, 217; P: 156, 180, 181, 184, 185

Philo (Judaeus), on the Logos, TP: 167

philosophers, ASP: 31, 32, 85; CH: 51; TM: 85, 86

phonograph, ASP: 64

phylacteries, JC: 90, 92; TT: 172, 173, 175

physical translation, KL: 69 (see *translation of body*)

physicians, ASP: 89, 104, 132; CH: 41, 69

physicist(s), ASP: 164, 165; CH: 31; P: 11, 13, 14; TP: 15, 108, 109

physics, P: 14

physiology, CH: 96, 99; TT: 147-149
  vs. metaphysics, on health, TT: 152-154

picture(s), mental, JC: 50-52 (see *thought picture*)

Pilate, Pontius, MJ: 161, 162

Pildash, MG: 186

pillar, MG: 272

"pinching", P: 167, 168

pineal gland, CH: 86, 87, 89; TM: 16, 31

spiritual, ASP: 17, 30, 31, 41, 47, 58, 67, 82; KL: 145;
  MG: 357, 368; MJ: 122; TP: 59, 81
through Holy Spirit, ASP: 41; KL: 153; TM: 61-70;
  TP: 53
through right thought and action, ASP: 45, 46; CH: 67;
  P: 150
to be invoked, JC: 16, 72, 155, 156, 188
Truth statements for realization of, JC: 37, 38;
  KL: 154; TP: 187, 188
twelve powers of Christ, KL: 113

powers of Being, (see *Being, powers of*)

powers, man as user and not possessor of God's creation
    and, TT: 92, 93

powers of man, KL: 112, 113, 117, 119; TM: 6, 49, 50,
    155; TT: 92, 93 (see *faculties of man; man, powers
    of; I AM, and development of man's powers*)
  training of, TM: 15, 16, 23, 34, 155

powers and nerve centers, (see *Body*)

practice, JC: 114

practicing presence of God (see *God, practicing presence
    of*)

Praetorium, MJ: 156

praise, and increase, CH: 80
  and prosperity, KL: 106, 180; TP: 34, 92
  center of, in body, CH: 75
  Christians and, JC: 138, 139
  consciousness enriched by, KL: 12; P: 35, 41, 105, 155;
    TP: 82, 90, 91 (see *consciousness, and praise*)
  healing and, JC: 57, 137-153
  importance of, in demonstration, CH: 78-80
  improves our work, CH: 79
  increases the good, CH: 79, 80; KL: 180; P: 82
  Judah as representing, CH: 74-76, 79; MG: 237, 275,

242

and supply, TP: 41

and thanksgiving, JC: 78, 137, 138; MJ: 111, 115; TP: 35, 43, 44, 82 (see *praise; thanksgiving, as way of prayer*)

and word, the power of, CH: 69; MJ: 76

answers to—why not always apparent, ASP: 126; CH: 18, 77, 80, 88, 128; JC: 47, 68, 85, 123-125, 175, 176; KL: 72; P: 93, 94

as an affirmation of Being, JC: 67

as communion, not asking for things, TP: 4, 5, 12, 13, 28, 29

as cumulative, CH: 78

as doorway to fourth dimension, KL: 170

as language of spirituality, KL: 10

as man's approach to God, TP: 21

as point of contact between God and man, ASP: 32; CH: 14, 15, 78; JC: 73, 123; KL: 16; TP: 4, 5, 12, 13, 21, 177

audible vs. silent, ASP: 11, 12, 28

begging vs. affirmative, P: 74-85

believing and receiving in, ASP: 104

cause of unanswered, CH: 80; P: 93, 94

character developed by, ASP: 32

Christians and, JC: 90

constructive words and, MJ: 76

daily, CH: 15; JC: 125, 169

defined, CH: 67; JC: 67, 70; TP: 3-5, 17, 28, 29

demonstration through (see *demonstration, through prayer*)

desire is form of, KL: 146; TP: 4

does not change God, KL: 146

dynamic character of atom and, ASP: 11, 12

effective, JC: 74

effects of, JC: 84

Emerson on, TP: 36

fasting and, KL: 4

for realization, and its consummation, JC: 47

for specific things, P: 101

freedom from debt through, P: 126, 129

group, ASP: 30, 31

how to offer, JC: 31, 74, 78-80; KL: 4-6, 9, 16, 71, 78,

245

prosperity through, TP: 33-37, 131, 178
realization and, ASP: 32; JC: 47; TP: 30, 34
redemption of body and intellect through, TP: 20, 26
related to laws of God, JC: 76
release of electronic energy by, TM: 5, 6
represented by Judah, MG: 237, 275, 300, 305, 331, 332, 337
resurrection of Jesus made possible by, MJ: 172, 173
scientific, ASP: 29, 126; KL: 170; TP: 24, 26, 157-163
silence and, ASP: 11; JC: 70; KL: 16; TP: 17
silent vs. audible, JC: 78, 79
spiritual understanding through, ASP: 32; KL: 4, 84; TM: 92, 123
supplication and, ASP: 11; CH: 18, 76; JC: 67, 69, 78, 83
supplication vs. thanksgiving in, CH: 75, 76
supplicative vs. affirmative, P: 74, 85; TM: 27; TP: 4, 28, 35, 159
supply and, ASP: 102; JC: 77, 78, 181; P: 31, 33, 73, 127, 128; TP: 13, 14
thought concentration and, ASP: 11, 12; JC: 70; TP: 31, 32, 81, 82
to God a communion of Father and Son, TP: 5, 13
turning to God within, for supply, P: 74
unanswered, MG: 175
unity with God through, TP: 177 (see *unity, with God*)
unselfish, MJ: 150, 151

Prayer, Lord's, JC: 67; KL: 72, 175; P: 31

prayer wheels, JC: 90, 92; TT: 173, 175

preachers, JC: 73

preaching, ASP: 42, 43; JC: 114; TM: 61; TP: 161, 162; TT: 141

precept, ASP: 42, 43

predestination, TM: 101, 102

psychic realm, MG: 37, 38, 93

psychoanalysis, TP: 90 (see *therapy*)

psychoanalysis and Shakespeare, ASP: 108

psychology, ASP: 56, 106-108, 112; CH: 42, 97;
    JC: 142-144, 155; KL: 75, 76; P: 49; TP: 30, 78

public work, MJ: 70

publishers, JC: 119, 120

punishment, CH: 123, 124; KL: 35

purification, KL: 191; MG: 187
    circumcision as indicative of, MG: 153, 154
    denial, of fasting, and, MG: 158; TT: 171
    fire and, MG: 168
    Gaham as representing, MG: 187
    Gihon as representing, MG: 37
    Ophir as representing, MG: 107
    Pool of Bethesda as representing, MJ: 57, 58
    thought as means of, TT: 153-155
    through punishment, CH: 124
    through regeneration, TM: 79, 80, 128, 167, 174
    Truth statements for realization of, CH: 60, 140, 141

Puritan fathers, TM: 113, 114

purity, ASP: 20, 36; JC: 103; MG: 48; TM: 92, 129,
    166, 167

purpose, TM: 57; TP: 45, 46 (see *prayer*)

purse, P: 114

Put, MG: 96

putting on Christ, (see *Christ, putting on*)

Q

quarrels, KL: 141, 175

Queen of Sheba, TP: 133

questions, JC: 23

quickening, P: 71, 104; TP: 75, 76
  spiritual, ASP: 43, 44, 66, 76, 99, 101, 107, 126;
    CH: 7, 35, 98; JC: 10, 16, 17, 103, 111, 112, 123,
    150, 191-193; KL: 16, 28, 34, 49, 158, 161, 162,
    168; MJ: 101, 102, 115, 173; P: 19, 32, 35, 48, 155;
    TM: 4, 15, 17, 19, 31, 44, 45, 61, 62, 88; TT: 147,
    148
  Truth statement for, CH: 40

quiet place, in man, JC: 80

R

Ra, MG: 355

Raamah, MG: 97

Raamses, (see *Rameses*)

rabbi, ASP: 26

rabble, MJ: 161

race, human, ASP: 29
  Adamic, KL: 98, 130, 131
  age of, ASP: 32, 70
  beliefs of, KL: 72, 79
  consciousness, (see *consciousness, race; Jesus, and race consciousness*)
  destiny of, ASP: 52, 53
  evolution of, (see *man, evolution of*)
  Jesus Christ and, KL: 130, 131; MJ: 123, 124, 169; TM: 138
  law and, KL: 131
  new, ASP: 28, 29, 31-34, 168, 169; CH: 90, 91; KL: 129, 189, 190; MJ: 149; TM: 3, 4
  resurrection is for every member of, KL: 97, 98
  thought, TM: 154

Rachel, CH: 75, 76; MG: 233, 235, 237, 238, 240-242, 244, 245, 252, 261, 262, 273, 275, 360, 361

radar, ASP: 65; MJ: 174

radiance, ASP: 81, 83, 84, 150, 151 (see *body, radiant; transfiguration*)

radiant body, (see *body, radiant*)

radiation, P: 12
  of mind, ASP: 14, 15, 40, 83; JC: 73
  of soul, JC: 17, 73, 110

radio, CH: 66; JC: 160; P: 10, 11; TM: 29, 30; TP: 75, 81

raiment, ASP: 22

rain, ASP: 9; KL: 179; MG: 33
  demonstration of, P: 33, 34, 100

rainbow, MG: 86, 87

"rainy day," P: 165, 166, 171, 172

ram, MG: 153, 183; TM: 26, 27

Rameses, or Raamses, MG: 355

ransom, ASP: 44

raven, MG: 83

rays, P: 12
  cosmic, P: 4, 5, 12
  healing, JC: 157
  light, P: 12
  radiant, P: 10
  X-, P: 12

Reader's Digest, ASP: 64

reading, JC: 118, 119; TM: 87, 88

realism, JC: 125

reality, ASP: 41, 57, 77-79, 96, 97, 123; JC: 101, 135; KL: 26, 63, 148, 160, 161; MG: 37; P: 27, 30, 39,

42, 49-52, 59, 81, 91, 122, 162; TP: 30, 130, 131
(see *Havilah*)

realization, JC: 105
  and prayer, ASP: 32; TP: 30, 34
  as expectancy objectified, JC: 50, 51
  as fourth dimension, KL: 170
  health and, JC: 39, 49; TP: 19, 118
  importance of, ASP: 60, 95
  meaning of, JC: 39, 40, 45
  prosperity and, P: 54, 55, 67, 85, 91, 98, 186
  spiritual, ASP: 28, 29, 32, 44, 60, 67, 77, 121, 127,
    157, 158; CH: 8, 81; JC: 13, 39-52, 83, 162, 176;
    KL: 78, 123, 146, 174, 190; P: 51; TP: 15, 18, 19,
    25, 28-31, 43-45, 47, 51, 139, 164, 172; TT: 170,
    171
  Truth statements to promote, CH: 17, 29, 38, 39;
    KL: 78

reaping, (see *sowing and reaping*) ASP: 48, 162

reason, TM: 45, 46, 88; TT: 117, 119
  human, ASP: 19

Rebekah, KL: 78; MG: 122, 186, 189, 194, 199, 200,
    208, 209, 213, 218-220, 225, 271, 323, 340, 341;
    TP: 140

rebellion, TT: 113

rebelliousness, CH: 128

rebirth, JC: 10, 52; TM: 80; TP: 15, 24; TT: 75 (see
    birth; born anew)

receiving, ASP: 104; P: 93 (see *giving*)

receiving from God, KL: 169

receptivity, MG: 236, 239, 275; MJ: 23, 56; TM: 28, 134,
    135, 156; TP: 114, 118, 154, 169, 172, 173; TT: 90

(see *hearing; giving*)
and healing, JC: 112, 113, 176, 177

red, MG: 210

redemption, ASP: 102; KL: 71, 95; MG: 115, 116, 151,
    152, 323; TT: 34 (see *man; prayer; regeneration;
    denial, as redeemer of man's consciousness*)
  is for mind, body, and soul, ASP: 131; KL: 95, 96;
    TP: 20, 26
  Jesus Christ and, ASP: 44; KL: 27, 124; TT: 115
  of body, ASP: 44, 124, 131; KL: 124-126; TM: 6, 7,
    69, 120, 174; TP: 20, 26
  of man, and work, JC: 98, 99
  of subconscious thoughts, ASP: 76

reembodiment, KL: 93, 94 (see *reincarnation*)

refining, ASP: 154

Reformation, Protestant, ASP: 129, 130

reform, CH: 126; JC: 54; KL: 32; P: 26, 118, 119, 147,
    148; TP: 29; TT: 7-9, 165

reformers, TP: 107

refuge, MG: 367

regeneration, MG: 9, 10, 52, 122, 137, 155, 184, 306, 353,
    357; TT: 154, 155 (see *body, regeneration of*)
  and obedience to Spirit, TT: 112, 113, 119
  and love, CH: 131, 132, 137, 138
  and Sermon on the Mount, TT: 86, 87
  and the mystical marriage, TM: 166, 167
  by superconscious mind, KL: 89, 91, 92
  Christ and, TT: 154, 155
  Christian and, JC: 193, 194; MJ: 35; TM: 174
  description of, CH: 131, 137, 138
  following Jesus Christ in, ASP: 38, 42, 43, 166; JC: 10,
    11, 52, 72, 83, 84, 97, 98, 163, 192; KL: 75, 163;

MG: 35, 71, 154; MJ: 18, 19, 109, 110; TM: 3, 15, 36, 37, 50, 61, 62, 65, 72-74, 76, 80, 90-93, 118-120, 135, 170; TP: 48, 64, 65, 110, 128; TT: 34, 35, 147, 148, 154

imagination's part in, TM: 71-82, 102, 103, 141
judgment and, TM: 133
love and, (see *love, and regeneration*)
method of, MG: 323, 339
of body, (see *body, regeneration of*)
only safe way to eternal life, KL: 74
purification of human life by, TM: 79, 80, 128, 167, 174
through appropriating Christ atoms, KL: 26, 132-134
transmutation and, MJ: 27
two states of mind at work in, MJ: 17, 18
union of spirit and body in, MJ: 24-26, 174
whole man—Spirit, soul, body—must be lifted up, KL: 93

Rehoboth, MG: 215

Rehoboth-Ir, MG: 99

reincarnation, ASP: 32, 116-121; JC: 13, 42; KL: 93-100, 160; MG: 90, 189-192, 364; MJ: 96, 97; TM: 120, 124, 138, 146, 171, 172; TP: 50, 51, 84, 149, 150; TT: 107, 156, 157, 159 (see *psychic phenomena*)
and Shakespeare, ASP: 107-109, 111, 112
body idea unchanged by, JC: 64; KL: 52; TM: 146
Christ and, TP: 149, 150
genius and, JC: 49; TM: 139
includes spirit, soul, and body, KL: 93
Jesus and, KL: 94; TM: 89, 174; TP: 72; TT: 150
of Hitlers, ASP: 53
partly to be speculated on, KL: 99
Paul and, ASP: 28, 120; JC: 13
when no longer necessary, KL: 28

rejoicing, TP: 105

rejuvenation, ASP: 101 (see *youth*)

relaxation, P: 168; TM: 159-160

religion, MG: 156; TT: 44 (see *science*)
  applied to development of cosmic mind for man,
    ASP: 59-61
  as way out of present chaos, ASP: 68, 69
  Christian, TT: 101-103, 132
  Christ Spirit vs. formal, JC: 184, 185; MJ: 35, 46, 98,
    99, 113, 152-156; P: 186, 187; TM: 110-129;
    TP: 124; TT: 11, 110, 132, 176
  economics and, P: 147, 186, 187
  evolution of, JC: 55, 126, 128, 142
  "inherited," MJ: 33, 34
  joy and, MG: 175
  made mysterious by priesthood, CH: 20, 21
  mind and, JC: 186, 187
  of Jesus Christ, JC: 94
  orthodox, TT: 101-103, 109
  psychology and, KL: 75, 76
  science of, CH: 18, 23-25, 30, 31, 43, 44, 67, 88, 89,
    135; KL: 37, 38; P: 56, 57, 145, 146; TP: 67;
    TT: 116 (see *science, religion as a*)
  spiritual vs. psychical world in, ASP: 112
  teachings of Jesus and, MG: 156
  vs. science, ASP: 40, 59, 60; CH: 67; P: 51, 57;
    TP: 98, 99
  zeal and, MJ: 29, 30, 153, 154

religionists, CH: 30, 31; TM: 142

remedies, TT: 152

renaissance, ASP: 33

renunciation, KL: 160, 161; MG: 78, 168, 192; P: 178;
    TM: 16, 21, 26, 142-160 (see *Thaddaeus*)

repentance, CH: 57, 58; JC: 59, 189, 190; KL: 141;
    MG: 337, 340; MJ: 35; TM: 142; TP: 174 (see *for-
    giveness*)

260

Solomon and, P: 77

rich man and Lazarus, (see *parable, of rich man and Lazarus*)

"rich men," P: 80, 163, 167; TT: 156-158

"righteous indignation," CH: 125, 126 (see *indignation, righteous*)

righteousness, ASP: 165; MG: 186; P: 16, 60, 80, 88, 90, 138, 139, 141; TP: 27

right hand of the Father, ASP: 27

"right side," MJ: 177

ring, MG: 270, 318; P: 61

Riphath, MG: 94

rites, religious, ASP: 54; P: 10

river, MG: 36, 37; TP: 150, 154
  of life, (see *life, river of*)
  of water of life (see *life, river of water of*)

robber, MG: 284; MJ: 100, 102

robe, seamless, P: 186

rock, CH: 68, 90, 91; MJ: 13; P: 42

Romans, MJ: 113

rooms, CH: 27, 28; P: 114

roots, TP: 19

Rosh, MG: 350

Rotherham, Joseph Bryant, TT: 87

"ruler of the feast," MJ: 27

rules, P: 29

Ruth, P: 65, 77

S

Sabbath, (see *rest*)
    as institution, KL: 171
    as state of consciousness, MJ: 59, 60
    how to keep, KL: 171, 172; MG: 31, 32; TM: 112-119
    Jewish, MJ: 164; TM: 112-115
    made for man, KL: 171
    what it is, KL: 171; MG: 31, 32; MJ: 59, 60

Sabtah, MG: 97

Sabteca, MG: 97

sacrament, ASP: 78, KL: 166, 167

sacrifice, KL: 95; MG: 58, 59, 143, 144, 178, 183, 184,
    252, 253; MJ: 123-125; P: 178; TM: 26, 27, 128,
    142, 152; TT: 167 (see *elimination; Jehovah*)
    privilege, KL: 95
    religious, JC: 55, 57, 162
    unto Jehovah, MG: 58, 59

sacrilege, ASP: 84; TT: 143

safety, ASP: 33, 53; JC: 21; TP: 112, 113

sages, ASP: 161

saints, JC: 76; P: 17, 20

salvation, MG: 146; TT: 150 (see *death, salvation from*)
    affirmation and, P: 180
    body included in, ASP: 157, 158
    dependent on consciousness, KL: 115; MJ: 49;
      TM: 118, 119; TT: 118, 119
    Jesus and, ASP: 159; JC: 132, 162, 165; KL: 93, 94,
      97; MJ: 46, 47, 51

Jesus Christ and, ASP: 73; JC: 165; KL: 20, 21, 167; MG: 139; MJ: 39; TM: 119; TP: 65; TT: 118, 132, 139, 140, 166, 167, 179
letter of law and, ASP: 26, 73; MJ: 66
mystery of, KL: 134
not yet fully understood, KL: 127
of all men, KL: 67, 93, 96, 97
of world, KL: 67
Paul on, TT: 167, 168
repentance and, TM: 142
Spirit and, ASP: 74; CH: 42; JC: 93, 94; MG: 139
through blood of Christ, KL: 134, 135; TM: 120; TP: 65
through obedience, (see *obedience, salvation through*)
through word, JC: 162, 175, 176

Salem, MG: 136

Salim, MJ: 41

salt, MG: 168; TM: 146

Samaria, MJ: 44; TP: 148, 151

Samlah, MG: 289

Samson and Delilah, TM: 36, 37 (see *Delilah*)

Samuel, TP: 117
Book of, TM: 24, 25

sanctification, MJ: 150, 151

sanctimoniousness, MJ: 87

sanctuary, ASP: 80

sandals, TM: 124

Sanhedrin, MJ: 34

Sarah, CH: 73, 74; MG: 140, 141, 148, 149, 151, 155, 159, 160, 172-179, 189, 191, 192, 204 (see *Abraham; Sarai; soul*)

Sarai, MG: 122, 140, 148, 155 (see *Sarah, soul*)

Satan, CH: 55, 56, 115, 116; JC: 20, 178; KL: 107, 131; MG: 48, 49; MJ: 123, 124; P: 96; TM: 70; TP: 101, 128; TT: 34, 114, 171, 172 (see *devil*)
  as adverse mind, TP: 128
  as adverse will, CH: 115, 116
  as experience, TT: 114
  as personal mind, CH: 55, 56
  as sensation, JC: 177, 178
  as the serpent, P: 96
    see also devil

Satan way vs. God way, MG: 48, 49

satisfaction, P: 92, 107, 108; TT: 60

Saul, or Paul, ASP: 26; MG: 151; TM: 74, 75, 92, 93 (see *Paul*)

Savior, MG: 366, 367; MJ: 41, 66, 87, 101, 102

Schaff, Philip, on the logos, TP: 167, 168

Schopenhauer, Arthur, TM: 83

science, and Genesis, JC: 188
  and metaphysics, JC: 44, 45
  Christianity as a, ASP: 31, 133; CH: 14, 23, 30, 31, 43, 44
  discoveries of, as aid to religion, P: 51. 52
  modern, vs. Christianity, ASP: 40, 56; JC: 142-144, 185
  vs. metaphysics, CH: 43, 44, 67, 68
  vs. religion, ASP: 85, 86
  of mind, CH: 11, 12; JC: 126, 127; TP: 81

of religion, (see *religion, science of*)
of spirit, CH: 7; KL: 42
on self-perpetuation of man's body, TT: 115
parallel between teaching of Jesus and modern, ASP: 56

Scofield, Rev. C. I., ASP: 98, MG: 150

Scriptural texts, (see *texts*)

Scriptures, JC: 177
and the listening ear, TP: 116
as portraying progress of mind, TT: 16
as record of man's experience, TP: 56
man's tendency to make idol of, TT: 103, 104
on light and intelligence, TT: 69; TP: 119, 120
on man and supermind realms, TP: 100
on man's power and dominion, CH: 50, 51
understanding of, and study of mind, JC: 54
see also Bible

Seba, MG: 96

second birth, CH: 26 (see *birth*)

"second coming of Jesus," JC: 12, 20, 149, 150

secret place, MG: 144, 145; TT: 72
as point of contact between man and God, TT: 72
of the Most High, ASP: 74; JC: 77; KL: 50; TP: 5, 81
(see *inner chamber*)

sects, JC: 99, TT: 109, 174

security, KL: 33; P: 56-58, 62

seed, ASP: 47, 59, 154; CH: 65, 137; JC: 28, 89, 112,
150, 194; MG: 27, 54, 357; MJ: 73; P: 67, 84, 104,
105, 117; TM: 39, 158; TP: 19, 106, 128, 172
as word of God, ASP: 59, 134-141 (see *man, as seed of
word of God*)

seeing, ASP: 56, 75; CH: 72 (see *good, seeing; sight*)

power and, ASP: 17; KL: 59; P: 96, 97, 148, 149;
TM: 6, 66, 89
vs. love, JC: 61, 62
vs. unselfishness, MG: 211

self-justification, JC: 70

selflessness, KL: 52, 53; MG: 234, 235

self-mastery, TP: 57

self-righteousness, JC: 70; MJ: 91; P: 119

selling, TT: 12

sensation, CH: 47, 56, 112; JC: 51; MG: 22, 24, 35, 36,
39, 45-56, 75, 365, 366, 368; MJ: 52; P: 97;
TM: 22, 23, 37, 41, 43, 57, 58, 145-147, 152, 157,
163, 165, 167-169; TP: 48, 52, 64; TT: 10, 30, 43,
45, 78, 82, 84, 86 (see *beasts; feeling; serpent; sex*)
and life, CH: 47, 56, 58
and prosperity, P: 19, 20, 97-98
and substance, MG: 22, 352; P: 13, 45-47, 51

sense, CH: 56, 130, 131; KL: 31, 32; MJ: 119 (see *consciousness, sense; man, sense; sensation*)
as center of will, KL: 62
consciousness, (see *consciousness, sense*)
delusions of, KL: 27, 61, 114
gratification of, JC: 130; KL: 50
Jesus came to rescue man from, KL: 171; MJ: 163
mind of, KL: 60, 62, 163
nature, TM: 121, 146
surrender to, KL: 31, 32
transmutation of, KL: 196
world, ASP: 21

senses, MG: 100, 162, 163; TT: 82, 157, 158

sensuality, MG: 120, 130, 135, 136, 161, 162

separation, TP: 134
   concerning, TP: 83, 84, 134, 158, 160, 161
   from God in consciousness, ASP: 40, 41, 135; CH: 15;
      KL: 33, 54; MG: 39, 44, 210, 211; MJ: 46, 168,
      169; TP: 14, 83, 84, 87, 158, 160; TT: 10, 15, 44
   from God is only seeming, JC: 25, 27, 36; MJ: 168, 169
   of mind and body, JC: 73

Sephar, MG: 107, 108

Serah, MG: 348

Sered, MG: 346

serenity, MG: 208, 213

Sermon on the Mount, TT: 86, 87

serpent, CH: 31, 34, 47, 112; MG: 45, 46, 49, 50, 53, 54,
    368; MJ: 24, 137, 140; P: 98; TM: 41, 43, 57, 167,
    168; TP: 64; TT: 59 (see *consciousness; sensation;
    sense*)

Serug, MG: 113

serums, TM: 147, 148, 157

servant, KL: 35; MG: 194, 200, 215; MJ: 115, 116 (see
    Jesus Christ as,)

service, TP: 161
   brings abundance, ASP: 35; P: 9, 150, 151
   in a universal sense, MJ: 149, 180
   Jesus and, MJ: 124; P: 150, 151
   to God, MG: 175; MJ: 119
   value of, MJ: 126, 127

Seth, MG: 65, 66, 68; TM: 99, 100 (see *balance*)

seven, (see *numbers*)
   lights, TM: 7

symbolical meaning of, MG: 358, 359; TP: 153, 154
to swear by the, MG: 181
wells, MG: 217

seven-day creation, ASP: 12

seventh day, TP: 182 (see *day, seventh*)

sex, MG: 47, 101, 129, 133, 134; TM: 166, 167 (see
Amorites)
and the tree of life, MG: 47-50
disease and depletion caused by indulgence in, TM: 22,
23, 57-59, 145-147, 165-169
lust, TT: 64 (see *lust*)

shade, TT: 158

Shakespeare, ASP: 50, 106-115, 128, 167; JC: 47, 48, 50,
51, 122, 166, 171, 188, 189; KL: 40, 41, 175; P: 13;
TM: 139; TP: 44, 45, 49, 97, 114, 118; TT: 28, 47
and healing, ASP: 112, 113
and reincarnation, ASP: 107-109, 111, 112
soul of, ASP: 106-115

Shammah, MG: 281

Shaul, or Saul, king of Edom, MG: 290
son of Simeon, MG: 344

Shaveh, MG: 136

Shaveh-kiriathaim, MG: 132

Sheba, queen of, P: 77; TP: 133
son of Jokshan, MG: 202, 203
son of Raamah, MG: 97

Shechem, city, MG: 120, 152, 264, 265, 269, 297
son of Hamor, MG: 265-269

sheep, ASP: 129; MG: 233, 306, 352; MJ: 57, 100, 103,

Shur, MG: 149, 171

sickness, (see *disease; disobedience; ills; sin*)
  avoid thoughts of, JC: 129, 173; TP: 104; TT: 116
  can be overcome through Truth, ASP: 101, 172;
    JC: 63, 64, 79, 100; TT: 56, 93
  cause of, ASP: 142; JC: 53, 57, 129; KL: 19, 64, 65,
    68, 134; TP: 148; TT: 20, 21
  does not exist in Truth, JC: 40
  how to overcome, JC: 89, 90, 129, 130, 143; TM: 106,
    107; TP: 82, 104, 105; TT: 93, 116, 130, 152
  Jesus and healing of, JC: 56-58; MJ: 57, 58, 60; P: 79
    (see *Jesus and healing*)
  Jesus Christ and healing of, JC: 56-58 (see *healing, Jesus
    Christ*)
  Truth statements for overcoming, JC: 64, 65, 173;
    TP: 104; TT: 152

Siddim, MG: 131

Sidon, MG: 100

sight, CH: 72, 76, 89; TP: 154 (see *eyes; Reuben*)

signs, JC: 79, 167; MJ: 105, 118

Silas, (see *Paul, and Silas*)

silence, ASP: 48, 148; KL: 10; MJ: 152; TT: 8 (see *communion; prayer*)
  and the still small voice, ASP: 148
  as doorway to fourth dimension, KL: 170
  as form of prayer, ASP: 11; JC: 70; TP: 17
  Carlyle on, TP: 21
  contacting God in, TP: 14, 18, 19, 27, 28, 32, 51, 59,
    81
  directions for employing, ASP: 74-76; JC: 111, 173,
    193; KL: 16, 18, 68; P: 151, 174; TP: 18-21, 59, 81,
    131, 136, 178; TT: 107, 144
  faithfulness in observing, TP: 35
  intellectual vs. spiritual, TP: 22-26

power and, TP: 81; TT: 8
prosperity, P: 15, 41, 54, 151
vs. noise, TT: 8

Silent Unity, TP: 92

silver, P: 14, 15, 161

Simeon, CH: 72 (see *hearing*)
   second son of Leah, MG: 236, 269, 275, 328, 344, 365, 366

Simon, MJ: 179; TM: 16, 28, 134, 135; TT: 90, 91 (see *Peter*)
   disciple of Jesus, JC: 56; MG: 151 (see *Peter; Simon Peter*)
   Magus, TT: 73
   Peter, CH: 73; JC: 83; TP: 118
   the Canaanite, MG: 241; TM: 140, 141
   the Cananaean, TM: 16, 22, 134, 135 (see *zeal*)
   the Zealot, TM: 140, 141; TP: 127

simple life vs. poverty, P: 106-108

simplicity, JC: 28, 125, 192

sin, KL: 44; MG: 53; MJ: 91; P: 184 (see *sickness; transgression*)
   all ills of humanity are result of, ASP: 131, 142, 147, 148, 151; JC: 12, 17, 53, 57-61, 173; KL: 32, 64, 65; MJ: 60; TM: 169; TT: 21, 46, 147, 154-157 (see *ills, mental and bodily, cause of*)
   as ignorance, MG: 90
   as mental transgression, P: 119, 120
   as missing the mark, CH: 90; JC: 161; TT: 48, 49
   denial of, CH: 57, 58; JC: 61, 103
   forgiveness of, CH: 57, 58; JC: 5, 58-60, 68; KL: 35; MJ: 17; P: 119; TP: 173, 174
   holding others in thought of, JC: 61
   Jesus Christ heals, MJ: 123
   Jesus saves from, ASP: 62; KL: 28, 29, 96, 131, 160;

smooth, MG: 220, 221

social conditions, ASP: 31

social service, JC: 55

sociology, JC: 55

Socrates, JC: 110, 147, 148; TM: 86

Sodom, TM: 146 (see *Bera; Gomorrah*)
   city of, MG: 102, 115, 136, 161-166, 168, 177, 178
   king of, MG: 137 (see *Bera*)

soil, ASP: 59

solar plexus, (see *plexus, solar; stomach*)

soldiers, MJ: 153

solids, JC: 172

Solomon, ASP: 80, 81; CH: 103; JC: 82; P: 34, 66, 77;
    TM: 46, 84, 85; TP: 132, 133; TT: 136
   and wisdom, TM: 46, 84; P: 77

Solomon's Porch, MJ: 103

Solomon's Temple, ASP: 80, 81; MJ: 96, 97

solvent, universal, TT: 153

Son, CH: 125, 126; JC: 16, 180; KL: 14-18; MJ: 88, 92,
   93, 130, 136; TT: 68, 70, 134, 141
   Father and, KL: 14-18; MJ: 16, 130; TT: 134 (see
   *Father, Son, and Holy Ghost; Father, Son, and Holy
   Spirit*)
   of God, ASP: 36, 42, 46, 99, 151, 157; JC: 10, 16, 17,
   19, 62, 191; KL: 52, 114, 115, 168; MG: 12, 26, 73;
   MJ: 15-17, 19, 39, 42, 61, 62, 76, 161-163, 168;
   P: 74; TM: 6, 40, 50, 118, 119, 145; TP: 15, 28, 41,

spending, P: 165, 170-172

spinal cord, MG: 305, 306; TM: 62, 167

Spinoza, JC: 171

Spirit, ASP: 24, 122; CH: 38, 96; JC: 92, 100, 103, 105, 107, 122, 193; KL: 11, 43; MG: 138; MJ: 150; P: 105; TM: 127; TT: 90, 106, 107, 127, 177 (see *God; God-mind*)
  activated by spoken word, ASP: 37, 38
  and consciousness, JC: 77
  and intuition and inspiration, CH: 7, 8, 10; JC: 96; P: 45, 46, 99; TM: 45, 77; TP: 50, 127, 130; TT: 113, 146 (see *Holy Spirit; intuition*)
  and prayer, TP: 4
  as accessible to all, JC: 92
  as bodily stimulant, P: 19
  as dominating mind force, KL: 9, 91
  as essence of all things, TP: 93-95
  as eternal, ASP: 151, 152; TM: 6
  as guide, ASP: 22, 75, 76, 111; KL: 43-53, 55, 66, 67, 91, 96, 175; TT: 110
  as healer, ASP: 67; P: 19
  as heaven, TM: 69
  as highest realm of mind, TT: 131
  as mind of God in executive capacity, JC: 180; KL: 99; TP: 67, 124
  as omnipresent, JC: 76, 78, 85, 89, 90
  as permeating all things, TT: 67, 96
  as potential man, soul and body, TM: 71, 138, 171, 172
  as principle, JC: 104; TT: 96
  as seat of power, CH: 10, 11
  as source of all that appears, ASP: 152; JC: 120, 137; KL: 77, 78; MG: 137, 138
  as source of prosperity, P: 46, 69, 126, 151, 160; TP: 92, 122, 123
  as source of soul and body, JC: 71, 72
  as source of strength, KL: 149; MG: 351; TM: 37-39, 123
  as state of consciousness, TT: 77

"still small voice," JC: 27, 28, 33, 126; MJ: 103, 104; TM: 43; TP: 17 (see *voice*)
  and communion, JC: 33

stimulants, affirmation for overcoming desire for, TM: 169

stinginess, CH: 53; P: 156

stinting, P: 170

stomach, ASP: 21; CH: 45, 52, 64, 111; TM: 16, 20, 49, 50, 134
  as seat of discrimination or judgment, TM: 16, 20, 49-50 (see *solar plexus*)
  Truth affirmation for healing, TP: 180

stones, CH: 120; KL: 83; MG: 37, 227-229, 264; MJ: 110, 111; P: 80, 81, 184, 185; TP: 128, 145 (see *rocks*)
  sermons in, JC: 40

storehouse of the Lord, P: 133

storms, TM: 148

Stratford upon Avon, England, ASP: 107, 108

stream, MJ: 152; P: 157

strength, MG: 64, 272, 362; MJ: 70, 71; P: 21, 160; TM: 34-40
  affirmation and, ASP: 50; KL: 150; TT: 150
  cattle as representing, MG: 40, 354
  David as representing, TM: 36
  defined, KL: 149
  derived from ideas of Divine Mind, ASP: 34; P: 9, 22
  Eliphaz as representing, MG: 279
  God, or Spirit, as source of, KL: 149; MG: 351; TM: 37-39, 123
  how to demonstrate, KL: 150
  Jesus and, KL: 149, 150; TM: 35-37

idea(s) of, CH: 44, 45; KL: 16, 170; MG: 33, 34, 45, 46, 287, 293; MJ: 73, 74; P: 18, 22, 24, 30, 31, 78
idea of, unsatisfactory if used without wisdom and love, P: 30
imagination and, MG: 293, 294, 329, 330; P: 49
increase of, MG: 68-70; P: 32, 35
Jesus and, ASP: 30, 31, 37, 38, 77, 78, 101, 167; CH: 86; JC: 41; MG: 369; MJ: 68-70, 74; P: 12, 46-48
Jesus Christ and, ASP: 44; JC: 147, 178; P: 78, 81
Joseph's dream about, MG: 295
Joseph's superior consciousness of universal, MG: 295
man is inlet and outlet of, CH: 22; KL: 69 (see man, as inlet and outlet of life, substance, and intelligence)
mental drawn from Christ, KL: 110
mind, KL: 106; MG: 293; P: 57 (see mind, substance and)
nature of spiritual, TP: 38-41, 145, 146, 159
   and its omnipresence, TP: 38-41
new concept of, MG: 127, 128
not to be limited by man, P: 101, 120
not to be used for selfish ends, P: 19, 20, 62
nucleated by idea, KL: 170
of Being, P: 57
of the body of flesh, ASP: 43
one primal, P: 32, 33, 91, 104, 140, 167; TT: 80
outer, P: 96
physical,
   part of God's, KL: 84
   waste of, KL: 163
race, starving for spiritual, KL: 133
release of, ASP: 101, 102
represented by money, KL: 106
sense and, P: 62
sensitive to man's thoughts, KL: 102
Spirit, ASP: 101, 102; TP: 30, 38-41, 94, 95, 122
source of incorruptible body, KL: 95
spiritual, KL: 11, 95, 96, 102, 133, 147, 183, 184; MG: 369; MJ: 51, 73, 75, 132, 133, 178; P: 15, 52-54, 99, 117; TM: 25, 122
strength and, MJ: 20

thought (etheric), TP: 122
thought shapes, CH: 44, 45; JC: 60; KL: 102, 103;
    P: 66-69, 98-100, 102, 103, 160, 167, 170, 177, 178;
    TP: 70, 71, 94, 95, 159; TT: 43, 153
transmutation of, JC: 145, 146
Truth statements for realization of, CH: 83, 84;
    KL: 14, 126, 184; P: 23, 25, 73, 79, 84, 91, 95, 100,
    102, 127, 159, 161, 164; TP: 41
two phases of, MG: 324, 325, 334
universal thought, JC: 60; P: 57, 162
uplifting of, MG: 137
waste of, KL: 163
words affect, ASP: 51

success, ASP: 74, 99, 104, 105, 128; CH: 85-91, 97, 127,
    128; JC: 100, 101, 113-115, 126, 134, 135, 175, 188;
    KL: 35, 46, 47, 140; MG: 308, 311, 325, 363;
    P: 19, 50, 57, 63, 64, 66, 77, 81, 82, 110, 112,
    138-140, 150, 151, 160, 161, 168; TM: 67, 68, 123,
    158-160; TP: 45, 46, 89, 111, 126, 127, 146, 147;
    TT: 11, 12, 26, 29, 93, 99, 100
as work of Spirit in man, MG: 308
faith as essential to, CH: 85-91
in business (see *business*) in world dependent on good
    judgment, CH: 127
Truth affirmation for realization of, P: 112
vs. failure, ASP: 105; MJ: 177

Succoth (place), MG: 263, 264

suffering, JC: 134; KL: 25, 29; MG: 36; P: 38, 153;
    TM: 107; TP: 21

suggestion, CH: 105; JC: 118, 119, 129; MJ: 101, 102;
    P: 107

suicide, mental, ASP: 46

sun, JC: 140, 171; MG: 19, 122, 308, 317, 355, 357;
    TM: 102, 103; TP: 48

sunshine, ASP: 66, 67; TP: 39

superconscious mind, (see *mind, superconscious*)

superconsciousness, ASP: 36-44 (see *mind, superconscious*)

superiority, false thought of, KL: 33, 66

superman, as thinking power, ASP: 61; JC: 16, 109; TM: 4; TP: 56, 68, 110 (see *Christ, as superman*)

supermind, (see *mind, super-*) (Christ mind)

supersensitiveness, TP: 50

superstition, ASP: 113

supersubstance, ASP: 23

supplanting, man's power of, MG: 211, 220, 223, 231 (see *Jacob, as supplanter*)

supplication, ASP: 11, 86; CH: 18, 76; KL: 72, 109; P: 74, 85; TP: 28, 29, 35, 158, 159 (see *prayer, supplication and*)

supply, P: whole book (see *abundance; plenty; prosperity*)
   adequate at all times, ASP: 136; JC: 134, 135; MJ: 177; P: 13, 15, 16, 20, 22, 31, 53, 54, 68, 74, 83, 85, 93, 164, 166
   and demand—law of, P: 18, 19, 53, 73, 93, 94 (and love, TT: 55)
   and Spirit substance, TP: 30, 38-41, 94, 95, 122
   and thanksgiving, (see *thanksgiving, as help in demonstration of supply*)
   as logical for Creator to provide for His creatures, P: 66
   consciousness of divine, P: 75, 79, 120, 128, 152, 169, 171
   dependent on faith, MJ: 180, 181; TP: 34; TT: 95, 96
   equalizing of, in new era, P: 23
   ether and, ASP: 10; P: 55, 90, 91; TT: 55, 61

faith and, ASP: 102; CH: 136; MJ: 180, 181; P: 20, 21, 94, 112

God as source of man's, ASP: 101, 102, 136, 137; CH: 34, 78, 136; JC: 18, 77, 78, 81, 120, 141, 178, 180, 181; MG: 251; MJ: 126, 178; P: 12-25, 30-35, 39, 54, 55, 60, 62, 77, 82, 83, 86, 111-114, 131, 132; TT: 94

gratitude and, MJ: 68, 69

hoarding and, JC: 68

imagination and, MG: 329, 330; P: 94; TT: 55

Jesus and, ASP: 101, 102, 136, 137; CH: 78; JC: 68, 69, 78, 81, 109, 134, 135, 139, 150, 181; KL: 102, 189; MJ: 68, 69, 177, 178; P: 12, 16, 34, 35, 38, 54, 62, 78-80, 84, 90, 91, 113, 132

(law of), JC: 81, 180; P: 32, 40, 53, 60, 67-86, 92-94, 126-128, 143, 164, 165, 169; TP: 122

love and, ASP: 35; TP: 34; TT: 55, 61

Mind and, (see *Mind, supply and; mind, supply and*)

mind and, (see *mind, supply and*)

praise and, CH: 78, 79; MJ: 68, 69; ASP: 102

praying for, ASP: 102; JC: 77, 78, 181; P: 31, 33, 73, 126, 128; TP: 13, 14

substance as, ASP: 101, 102, 136, 170; KL: 101, 102; P: 12-25, 159

word of God and, ASP: 136, 137

zeal and, CH: 78, 79

suppression, CH: 114, 115 (see *self-control*)

surgery, TM: 148

suspicion, P: 118

swear, (see *oath*)

sweat, KL: 62

sword, MG: 58, 96, 364

Sychar (city), MJ: 44, 49

symbolism, ASP: 12, 19, 77, 80, 81, 83, 162, 163; CH: 58, 62, 73, 74; JC: 20, 141, 150-153; MG: whole book; MJ: 12, 24-27; TM: 7, 70, 77, 79, 89, 97, 133-135, 151-153; TP: 66-68, 97, 139-145, 149-154 (see *Bible; symbology; symbols*)
of child, MG: 29; P: 113

symbology, ASP: 19, 31, 161; CH: 72, 73; KL: 97, 133, 134; TM: 77, 81, 89, 97, 133; TP: 66, 67, 97 (see *allegory; symbolism; symbols*)

symbols, ASP: 26, 77, 80, 161, 162; CH: 72, 114, 120; JC: 20, 149, 150; KL: 133; TM: 133, 134; TP: 97 (see *symbolism; symbology*)

sympathetic nervous system, JC: 178

sympathy, JC: 27; P: 68, 69; TM: 20

synthetics, JC: 120

syphilis, TM: 145

T

Tabernacle, ASP: 80, 81
  of the Israelites, as symbol of man's body, ASP: 80, 81

tabernacle, ASP: 156; MG: 120; MJ: 96; TM: 25

table of the Lord, JC: 158, 159

Tahash, MG: 187

talent, JC: 135; MJ: 137

talents, KL: 112; P: 81, 82
  a lesson in prosperity, P: 81, 82
  hindrances to expression of, KL: 112
  parable of, P: 81, 82

talk, KL: 47; P: 126
  negative, P: 13, 103, 104, 115

Tamar, MG: 306, 307

Tarshish, MG: 95

Tarsus, Asia Minor, ASP: 26

taste, TP: 153, 154
  good, JC: 120

"teacher in Israel," P: 45

teacher, ASP: 59, 60, 103, 106; MJ: 127; P: 153; TP: 31,
    32 (see *Jesus Christ as helper and teacher*)

teachings, (see *Jesus, teachings of*)

Tebah, MG: 187

tenth, P: 131 (see *tithe*)

Terah, MG: 118

teraphim, MG: 248-250, 252

testifying for the Lord, ASP: 39

testimonials, Unity, ASP: 131, 132, 133

texts, list of scriptural, used as affirmation and denials,
CH: 17, 29, 39, 48, 49, 60, 70, 71, 82-85, 94, 95,
106, 118, 119, 129, 130, 139-141 (see *affirmations
and denials*)

Thaddaeus, (renunciation), called also Lebbaeus, TM: 16,
21, 158 (see *Lebbaeus; renunciation*)

thanks, JC: 138

thanksgiving, P: 155 (see *joy; praise; prayer*)
and prayer (see *prayer, and thanksgiving*)
as help in demonstration of supply, ASP: 102; CH: 78;
KL: 106; MJ: 67, 68, 69; P: 69, 84, 105, 142 (see
demonstration through prayer, thanksgiving)
as means of developing spiritual consciousness, ASP: 28;
MJ: 68, 69; P: 34, 35
as way of prayer, CH: 76; MJ: 115; TP: 43, 44
freedom from debt through, P: 124, 125, 129
health gained through, JC: 137-153; MJ: 67, 111;
P: 82; TM: 144; TP: 82
Jesus and, JC: 78, 86; MJ: 68, 69, 111; P: 84, 105
power in, MJ: 68; P: 46, 47

theology, vs. metaphysical doctrine, TT: 67, 68

theory vs. works, TT: 68

therapy, spiritual soul, TP: 90-92

thief, CH: 58, 59; MJ: 100, 102; TM: 22

"thief and a robber," MJ: 100

things, ASP: 88; TM: 155
    all are in God as potentialities, JC: 67
    all, new, TT: 125, 126
    all visible, had origin in invisible, ASP: 50, 84; P: 41,
      129
    are affected by praise, CH: 48, 49
    are evidence of intelligence and power, ASP: 135
    creeping, MG: 24, 33
    do not make happiness, CH: 90
    formed, JC: 35, 41, 50 (see formed, the)
    God is source of all, ASP: 59, 93, 97
    have spiritual side, P: 147
    increased by praise and thanksgiving, P: 105
    Jesus on, JC: 78, 134, 135; P: 81
    material, KL: 61
    "not seen," TP: 27; P: 141
    originate in ideas, ASP: 94, 97; CH: 103; JC: 71;
      P: 32, 33, 77, 80, 81, 162
    originate in mind, JC: 147; MJ: 26
    shall be added, TP: 27; P: 141
    spiritual, JC: 139
    thoughts are, TP: 96-99

thinking, KL: 52, 53, 63, 191; TM: 37; TT: 26, 52-57,
    63, 89, 90, 164 (see thought)
    aimless, JC: 43
    and plenty, (see plenty, thinking and)
    bridges gulf between religion and science, CH: 30, 31
    defined, ASP: 94; TT: 96
    faculty located in head, KL: 113
    God-Mind in man is, ASP: 99, 100; CH: 19, 23, 24, 98;
      JC: 40
    Jesus and, JC: 54
    relation between eating and, ASP: 72, 73
    Shakespeare on, ASP: 114
    spiritual body formed through, MG: 264; TT: 86
    Truth affirmations for right, CH: 48, 49
    vs. day-dreaming, CH: 96

thirst, MJ: 81

Thomas (understanding), CH: 116; JC: 111, 184, 185;
    MG: 239, 240; MJ: 107, 131, 171; TM: 16, 21, 91,
    104 (see *understanding*)

thorn, MG: 373

thought(s), KL: 17, 77, 78, 97, 98; MG: 104, 249, 250;
    MJ: 91, 144; TM: 122 (see *sheep; thinking*)
  about Truth, KL: 12
  act originates in, TT: 9
  affinity of, MJ: 135
  affirmation for controlling, (see *thoughts, Truth affirma-*
    tion for control of)
  and cells, (see *cells, and thought*)
  and character, JC: 16, 176
  and consciousness, ASP: 94, 95, 118, 119; JC: 33, 81,
    82, 84; KL: 65, 67; TP: 90, 91, 170; TT: 52, 53, 86,
    165, 168
  and demonstration, JC: 15, 89, 104, 105, 106, 112,
    118, 119, 120, 127, 128; MJ: 115, 139; P: 57-86, 92,
    93; TP: 74; TT: 29, 116 (see *thought, demonstrating*
    Christ by)
  and effect, ASP: 19, 81, 129, 139, 140 (see *thought,*
    effect of, on body; on mind and nerves)
  and emotion, in relation to nervous system, TM: 133,
    134
  and energy, ASP: 14; JC: 19, 39, 43, 93, 94, 104, 105,
    138
  and expression, MG: 45
  and habit, TM: 129
  animals as representing, TM: 81, 122
  and love, CH: 130, 138; KL: 30, 34; MJ: 180;
    TP: 114, 115; TT: 56, 57
  and manifestation, ASP: 94, 118, 119; TP: 90, 91 (see
    manifestation, thought controls)
  and microbes, TT: 18-27
  and order, JC: 121
  and persistence, P: 33, 34, 65, 71, 72, 112, 113, 114
  and spiritual substance, P: 15, 52, 53, 54, 99, 117

and spoken word, CH: 63, 64, 68; MJ: 54, 55; P: 36;
   TP: 73, 74, 91
and will, CH: 109, 116
and word, TP: 73, 74
as basis of external conditions, MJ: 177
as builder of nerves and brain centers, TM: 136
as cause, ASP: 48; JC: 15, 16, 47, 48, 189; MG: 45;
   MJ: 30, 177; P: 26, 40; TM: 19, 73, 79, 80, 81, 93,
   135, 143, 146, 158
   of poverty or prosperity, P: 13, 21, 26, 52-54, 67, 68,
      69, 80, 93, 98, 108, 114, 115, 118-129, 152, 157,
      183; TP: 34
as director of body forces, ASP: 43, 72, 76, 113, 118,
   119, 121; TM: 142, 143
as eternal reality, P: 43
as formative vehicle to express divine ideas, ASP: 93, 94;
   CH: 63, 64
as God's only mode of manifestation, TT: 8
as greatest gift of God to man, KL: 147
as process by which abstract is made concrete, ASP: 94,
   99; CH: 99
as quickener of life force, JC: 104, 105; P: 71, 72
as seed, ASP: 47
as Son of God and son of man, CH: 50
as source of disease, ASP: 148; TM: 103, 134, 145,
   146, 148 (see *disease, thinking body into*)
as subject to man, ASP: 19
as transformer of man's body and world, ASP: 32, 43,
   51, 52, 124, 143, 146, 147, 148
as working power of mind, JC: 110; KL: 38, 64, 65, 77,
   78, 102, 113-117, 125, 141, 153
ascending, MJ: 167, 169
atmosphere, MJ: 30, 31
attainment depends on right, ASP: 24; KL: 167
attitudes and, KL: 34
body as fruit of man's, TT: 116
body is built through, ASP: 37, 74, 75, 94, 119, 121;
   CH: 43, 98, 99; JC: 40, 41; KL: 180; TP: 73, 74;
   TT: 116, 147
bondage to personal, MG: 330
breaking up of old structures of, JC: 62, 63, 184, 185,

189, 190

burdensome, MG: 266, 267, 297, 298

can be transformed or dissolved, P: 117, 118, 148, 174, 175

centers of, in body, CH: 45-47, 74, 75, 96, 97, 98, 99, 100

change of, necessary to healthy mind, TM: 142-145

Christ body formed through, KL: 10, 11, 28, 63; TT: 62, 63 (see *Christ, body*)

concentration of, ASP: 11, 12; CH: 115; JC: 70; MG: 117; TP: 31, 32, 81, 82

conditions are formed by, CH: 63, 64, 100

congestion, TM: 144 (see *congestion*)

consciousness formed by, JC: 33; TT: 54, 71, 106, 152

constructive, JC: 54; TP: 82, 101

control of, ASP: 28, 148; CH: 50-59, 115; KL: 74, 75, 77, 114-119, 153; TP: 40, 110, 111, 138, 139, 178; TT: 91 (see *mastery*)

   Truth affirmation for, KL: 121

corresponds to Holy Spirit in Divine Mind, ASP: 99

creating new atmosphere of, JC: 84, 192

creations, TM: 71

creative, TP: 74

criticism and, TP: 114

crystallization of, TT: 165

demonstrating Christ by, ASP: 70-79, 120, 124, 148; TT: 148

destructive, KL: 75, 119; MJ: 32; TM: 79, 103, 134, 146, 148, 158, 159; TP: 82, 101

   remedy for, P: 149

divided, MG: 202

double standard of, MG: 297, 298

each, is an identity that has a central ego, CH: 50

effect of,

   on body, ASP: 81, 119, 121; CH: 34, 40, 41, 45, 46, 54, 69, 99, 100, 101, 104, 122, 123, 132; JC: 40, 41, 44, 53, 127, 128, 129, 138, 139, 175; KL: 95, 180, 193; MG: 71; TM: 37, 129, 142, 143, 156; TT: 147, 151

   on mind and nerves, CH: 40, 64, 130, 138; KL: 180

elements controlled through, ASP: 9; KL: 179 (see

Elijah, and control of elements)
endure after body is dissolved, JC: 189
error, ASP: 149; CH: 57, 138; JC: 60; MG: 72, 75, 78,
    79, 84, 135, 165, 166, 179, 283, 289; P: 175;
    TT: 34, 54, 55, 104, 162
error, and its effect on love, TT: 54, 55
every, has entity, P: 118, 121
every ill traced to sinning, ASP: 148
every, should be placed under divine law, JC: 121
everything in universe is product of, JC: 186
exploiting the negative mass, ASP: 128
faith and, ASP: 74; KL: 110-121; TT: 90
force, JC: 45, 84; creating harmful, by condemnation,
    CH: 122, 123
forgiveness and, JC: 60, 61
formative power of, CH: 40-48, 62, 63, 75, 92, 98, 99;
    JC: 39, 60, 112, 127, 128, 143, 176; KL: 16, 19, 63;
    MG: 71, 325; TM: 121, 143, 144; TP: 94, 95, 98
formed, MG: 45, 349 (see *imagination; Tiras*)
freedom of, TT: 104
generated by mind, TT: 8, 18, 19, 116
goat, ASP: 46, 47, 49
God creates through, CH: 18, 19
good, ASP: 47, 48; TT: 34
    vs. bad, ASP: 28, 45, 114; MG: 347; MJ: 63, 105;
        TM: 121 (see *good, vs. evil*)
habits of, MG: 72, 162; P: 60
healing forces stirred by, JC: 18, 19, 40, 49, 59, 60,
    127, 128, 129, 170, 192, 193; MG: 125
heaven and hell as results of one's own, ASP: 97
holding a, P: 71
images, KL: 63; TM: 77, 80; TP: 70-72
imagination and, TM: 73
impermanency of error, ASP: 49
inheriting kingdom of good, ASP: 47
intellectual vs. spiritual, MJ: 112, 113, 114, 164
is thing, P: 175; TP: 96, 99
Jesus and, ASP: 10; JC: 138; KL: 28, 185; MG: 71;
    MJ: 135; TP: 76; TT: 124, 164, 168, 170
Jesus Christ and, JC: 129; P: 148; TT: 148, 164
law of, CH: 24, 30, 31, 122; JC: 121; MJ: 26; P: 59;

treatment, metaphysical, ASP: 67, 82, 89; CH: 36, 53, 66, 110, 111, 112, 113, 115, 116, 121, 125, 126, 127, 129, 131, 138; JC: 37, 42, 52, 113, 118, 127, 128, 183; KL: 20, 22, 64, 65; MG: 122; P: 154; TP: 91, 92, 178-188; TT: 25, 44, 56, 59, 118-121, 143 (see *healing, metaphysical; prayer*)
  shock, ASP: 67
  six day, TP: 182-188

treatments, (see *Prayer treatments*)

tree, MJ: 36
  fig, KL: 73
  fruit of the, TM: 168
  "in the midst of the garden," CH: 34; MG: 35, 38, 39, 49, 52; TM: 168 (see *tree of life*)
  oak, JC: 28; MG: 120, 152, 157, 192, 193
  of knowledge of good and evil, CH: 55-57; JC: 178; KL: 54, 73, 74; MG: 35, 39; MJ: 36; TM: 153
  of life, CH: 34, 47; KL: 73, 74; MG: 35; TM: 62; TT: 96, 151 (see *tree "in the midst of the garden"*) in Genesis, interpreted, CH: 47

trenches, P: 100

trial, MG: 36, 177

tribes of Israel, CH: 120; TM: 3

tribes, twelve, JC: 152

trickery, KL: 85

Trinity, TT: 134
  and the twelvefold man, TM: 99
  as God, Christ, man, TM: 99
  as spirit, soul, and body (or spirit, consciousness, and substance), MG: 157, 158, 165
  as threefold nature of man, TM: 45
  explained, CH: 20, 21
  in all creative processes, P: 4

God as, JC: 30
grasped first by intellect, P: 45, 57, 58
has origin in Divine Mind, KL: 19
idea of, represented by Joseph, MG: 339
importance of adhering to one system of, JC: 19
logic of, KL: 19
loyalty to, P: 65
man cut away from, KL: 114
meditation on, KL: 12
no copyright on principles of, ASP: 38
no need to prove absolute, MJ: 32
no sickness in, JC: 40
of Being, JC: 60; KL: 125; P: 19, 63, 180
overcoming through, ASP: 38, 39
partaking of body and blood of Jesus Christ by appro-
    priating ("eating") words of, ASP: 78, 169
possibility of expressing, JC: 133, 134
practical application of, CH: 21, 22; MG: 105
relative vs. absolute, ASP: 88
religious and mystical systems vs. practical demonstra-
    tion of, CH: 21, 22
revealed individually, JC: 98
science of, CH: 18
seamless garment of Jesus a symbol of, MG: 294, 295;
    MJ: 162
Spirit of, (see *Spirit, of Truth; Spirit, of truth*)
statements of, ASP: 152; JC: 130; P: 185
testifying in favor of, TT: 69
value of statements of, JC: 130
word of, JC: 81-91, 111
words of, JC: 87-91, 111; P: 105, 106; TP: 20
worked into body through thought, KL: 125

truth, ASP: 96; CH: 32, 33; JC: 91, 133; P: 29, 76;
    TT: 116
absolute, ASP: 88
of Being, ASP: 40; CH: 10, 55, 115
perception of, is intuitional, KL: 48, 49
spiritual, TT: 140, 174 (see also *Jesus; Principle; Spirit
    of Truth*)

U

ultraviolet rays, ASP: 66, 67

unclean, TM: 78, 79

unction, divine, ASP: 66, 67

underconsumption, P: 23

understanding, CH: 74, 97, 98, 126; JC: 59, 60, 61, 74,
    76, 173; MJ: 110, 146; P: 35, 61, 62, 179, 180;
    TM: 122; TP: 62, 81, 82 (see *intelligence; knowl-
    edge; light; Manasseh; Thomas; wisdom*)
  affirming for, KL: 156, 166
  and the All-Presence, CH: 67
  and will, MG: 20, 319, 320
  as first requisite for patience, KL: 181
  as fruit of Spirit's inspiration and knowledge, KL: 127,
    156, 157 (see *Spirit, understanding*)
  Asher as symbolizing, MG: 239, 276
  breath of Almighty gives, CH: 7
  Christ cleansing of, MJ: 127
  claiming, CH: 113, 114; KL: 156
  day as representing, MG: 81
  divine, P: 153
  Enaim and, MG: 306
  faith and, CH: 37; JC: 72; MJ: 81; P: 45, 84
  feet as representing a phase of, P: 61
  fruit of Spirit's inspiration and knowledge, KL: 157
  Gentiles as representing material, MJ: 49
  growth in, JC: 48, 111; MG: 274, 298
  how attained, JC: 98, 196; MG: 139, 259; P: 52
  illumined, MG: 106
  imagination and, MJ: 22; TM: 101
  intellectual, ASP: 56, 77; KL: 155; MJ: 107; TM: 88,
    89, 90, 91, 104
  interrelation between wisdom, knowledge, and,

law of, TT: 24, 25
mental, MG: 23
spiritual, (mastery through), ASP: 40; JC: 19; KL: 37,
   38, 139-197; MG: 23; TP: 4, 58, 59, 66-69

unformed, the, CH: 36; MG: 23 (see *formless, the; sea*)

unhappiness, ASP: 75

union, (love), MG: 236, 237, 275, 365, 366

United States, P: 58, 127, 187

unity, MG: 333, 334; MJ: 150, 151, 180; TM: 151 (see
   oneness)
  Cheran represents phase of, MG: 287
  idea of, JC: 130; KL: 151, 152
  in Spirit, ASP: 78
  law of, MG: 261
  love and, JC: 61, 62; KL: 151, 152; P: 65 (see *love, as
     unifier*)
  of God, man, and universe, ASP: 153
  of man and his body, ASP: 29
  of man and his world, ASP: 29
  of mind and body, KL: 82, 97; MG: 263
  of mind and elements, ASP: 29
  of Spirit, soul, and body, ASP: 153
  of the race, in Christ, JC: 61, 131
  on evolution of soul and body, TP: 66, 67
  realization of divine, MJ: 122, 151
  spiritual work of, ASP: 54, 55
  Truth affirmation for, KL: 163
  with God, ASP: 29, 37, 38, 41, 43, 68, 69, 84, 104,
     122; CH: 14, 15, 25, 35, 37, 42, 52, 63, 66, 67, 74,
     76, 81, 102, 120, 131; JC: 21, 40, 50, 131, 143, 144,
     196; KL: 178; MJ: 146, 173; P: 45; TM: 27, 50, 65,
     105, 184, 185; TP: 16, 20, 24, 25, 43, 63, 88, 177
  Ohad as symbolizing, MG: 344
  with Jesus Christ, TM: 115
  with Spirit, KL: 11, 18; MJ: 122; P: 31; TP: 20, 124,
     125; TT: 84, 141, 151

with the Father, KL: 10, 27, 29, 32, 33, 77, 154, 178; MJ: 131, 132, 134, 147, 149; P: 75; TP: 93 (see *Father, Jesus' unity with*)

Unity School—spiritual work of, ASP: 91, 92

universal man, KL: 110 (see *man, universal*)

universal Mind, (see *Mind, universal*)

universal mind, (see *mind, universal*)

universal will, (see *God's will*)

universe, ASP: 91, 92, 160; CH: 51, 135; JC: 27, 149, 187; KL: 21, 22, 158; MG: 28, 59; TP: 71
all belongs to God, P: 138
as body of God, JC: 161
as God's symphony, ASP: 115; JC: 171
as product of thought, JC: 4, 33, 186, 187
destiny of, ASP: 85
existed billions of years in past, KL: 130
Jesus understood God's, ASP: 56
law as foundation of, JC: 129, 172; MJ: 36; P: 93
Mind as reservoir of, ASP: 91, 93; CH: 14, 61; JC: 28, 29, 100, 101, 127
nature of, KL: 158
no cessation in activity of, TM: 112, 113, 120
originated in mind, TM: 143
resolved back into original essence in God, MG: 59
secret of, JC: 129
spiritual, JC: 96
understanding of, CH: 19; KL: 130

unknown God—altar to, KL: 146

unmanifest, the, TM: 52

upliftment, spiritual, ASP: 152, 153, 154

"upper chamber," ASP: 30, 31

"upper room," ASP: 66; CH: 27, 28, 75; P: 48, 61; TM: 27, 135 (see *inner chamber*)
and the receiving of power from the Holy Spirit, P: 48 (crown or top of head), CH: 27, 28, 75, 76; P: 61
place of contact between Divine Mind and man's mind, TM: 27, 135
See also "Inner Chamber"

Ur (of the Chaldees), MG: 113

uranium, ASP: 50, 51

Urim and Thummim, meaning of, CH: 120

urinary disorders, Truth statement for healing, TP: 181

use, MJ: 137

usefulness, P: 150, 151

Utopia, (see *Babel*)

Uz,
son of Aram, MG: 104
son of Dishan, MG: 288

Uzal, MG: 106

V

vacation, P: 106

vaccination, TM: 147

vacillation, CH: 124, 125

Valley of Hinnom, (see *Gehenna; Hinnom, Valley of*)

Vanderbilt, KL: 47

vanity, JC: 103; P: 17

vegetarianism, ASP: 51, 122

vengeance, MG: 266, 269, 366

venison, MG: 209

vessels, P: 113, 114

vibration(s), ASP: 54, 57, 64, 65, 66, 165, 166;
CH: 62-65, 68, 69; JC: 170, 172, 174; KL: 38, 65;
P: 36; TM: 133, 134, 141; TP: 43, 50, 74, 75
  change in race, ASP: 165, 166
  destructive, of atomic forces, ASP: 65, 66
  effects of thought and word, CH: 62-65, 68, 69
  sound, ASP: 57
  trumpet and voice, ASP: 54, 55

vice unmentionable, MG: 162

victory, MG: 136, 306

vineyard, MG: 88

violence, TM: 121

virtue, MG: 269

visible, the, ASP: 50, 134; KL: 102; P: 27, 28; TP: 30

vision, (sight), MG: 236, 274 (see *Reuben*)

visions, TP: 51, 52; TT: 136, 137 (see *dreams; imagination*)
  interpretation of, MG: 294, 317; TM: 72, 77, 81
  man may be taught by, CH: 114; KL: 155; MG: 139, 219, 220, 228; TM: 74, 75, 77; TP: 51; TT: 136
  of Abraham, MG: 145, 151, 152
  of Ananias, TM: 75, 76
  of Jacob, MG: 228; TT: 136 (see *Jacob, dreams of*)
  of Joseph, MG: 293
  of Paul, CH: 102, 103
  of Peter, TM: 78, 79; TT: 137; CH: 103
  of Saul, TM: 76

visualization, ASP: 64; P: 84, 101

vitality, ASP: 66; JC: 104, 146; MG: 121; MJ: 25, 27, 67, 69; P: 19; TM: 37; TP: 20; TT: 41, 47

vitamins, TM: 136, 157, 158

voice, JC: 170, 172; KL: 74, 75, 153; MJ: 103, 104, 111, 112; TM: 30, 43, 62, 63, 64, 65; TP: 58, 116, 117 (see *Word*)
  affirmation for strengthening, KL: 75
  See also word

voices, inner, ASP: 56, 57, 148

voltage of thoughts measured, ASP: 14, 15, 30

Voltaire, KL: 24

Vulgate, the, ASP: 83

W

mind, JC: 160
radio, JC: 159, 160

Way-Shower, (see *Jesus, as way-shower*)

Way, the, KL: 36, 57, 164

way, the, MG: 283; P: 32

weakness,
  cause of, CH: 45, 46, 54, 64; KL: 19
  denial of, KL: 150
  healing of, CH: 80; P: 71; TM: 38; TP: 181; TT: 150

wealth, (see *money; riches*)
  and kingdom of heaven, P: 16, 166, 167
  hoarding vs. circulation of, P: 89, 90, 166, 167
  ideas and, P: 77, 94
  imagination and, P: 95, 96
  in consciousness, P: 56
  inequalities of, based on desire for personal possession,
    P: 16, 17, 127, 128 (see *money*)
  Jehovah promised, P: 161
  material, TP: 38
  of mind, P: 87
  true source of, JC: 49; KL: 101-109; P: 13, 14-25,
    30-41, 77, 94, 104, 109, 110, 171
  widespread desire for, P: 161-164, 167
  worship of, P: 182

weapons, MJ: 152; P: 184

weather, TM: 149, 150

web, spider's, TT: 166

Webster, JC: 28, 29; P: 87

weeping, MG: 71

well, MG: 149, 180, 181, 205, 214, 215, 217, 233; MJ: 47

(see *Jacob's well; water*)

Wesley, John, TT: 109

west, MG: 35

wheat, P: 139

white, TP: 123

wholeness, principle of, JC: 9, 24, 39, 182; MG: 149 (see
    Spirit)

widow, ASP: 10, 125; KL: 103, 104; P: 99, 113, 134,
    135; TP: 33, 34

widow's mite, MJ: 143, 144

wife, MG: 226

wilderness, ASP: 143; KL: 78; MG: 179; TM: 121, 122;
    TP: 140

will, TM: 62, 97-109; TP: 182
    Abimelech as representing phase of, MG: 216
    adverse, CH: 115; MG: 73 (see *devil*)
    and body, CH: 37, 111
    and health, CH: 115
    and thought, CH: 109, 116
    antidote for a dictatorial, KL: 30, 31; TM: 59
    as basic force in creation, ASP: 19
    as blind without intelligence, TT: 78, 79
    as center of action, TM: 97; TP: 182
    as divine idea, CH: 107, 108
    as ego, MG: 42
    as executive faculty of mind, CH: 116; KL: 61, 62,
        156, 157, 194; TM: 105
    as used by Jesus, P: 78, 79
    concentration of, JC: 188
    difference between seeming and pure, KL: 62
    divine, CH: 33, 37; JC: 77; MG: 19, 20, 349, 350

dominating, CH: 53; KL: 50; TP: 68
domineering, symbolized in Herod, KL: 50
effect of, on body, CH: 37, 111
egotism and, MG: 144
Ephraim as representing, MG: 319, 320, 362, 363
executive power of mind, KL: 156, 194
false, KL: 62
free, CH: 35, 55, 108, 109; JC: 177; KL: 29, 55;
   P: 58, 59, 77; TM: 101, 102, 103, 104, 105, 109;
   TP: 69; TT: 104
freedom of, KL: 29, 55
front of brain as seat of, MJ: 162; TM: 59, 62, 159
has power over matter, JC: 188
highest aspect of, KL: 145
human, MG: 19, 20, 97, 148, 172, 173, 180, 181, 258,
   259
I AM and, CH: 34, 108, 109, 116; KL: 145; TT: 29, 79
imagination and, MG: 359; P: 77, 78
is the man, KL: 145
Jesus Christ and divine, CH: 33
man as God's, individualized, KL: 110 (see man, as will
   of God)
man, the will of Christ, KL: 110
Matthew as representing, CH: 116; MJ: 107; TM: 16,
   21, 22, 97-109
not to be retarded or broken, CH: 109, 110, 112
of God, CH: 18, 19, 76, 77; TM: 39 (see Jesus, and will
   of God)
of the Father, MJ: 74, 75
personal, JC: 112; MG: 148, 213, 290, 370; MJ: 153;
   TP: 150-153
   as detrimental to bodily health, TP: 150-153
   vs. universal, TM: 107, 108
perverted, CH: 111
prosperity demonstrated through, P: 111, 112
relaxation of, TM: 158, 159, 160
self-control and, CH: 114, 115 (see self-control)
should not be broken, CH: 109, 112
submission to another's, CH: 113; TM: 107, 109
symbolism of, MG: 54, 55, 143, 144
to strengthen the, CH: 110, 111, 112, 113; P: 111

and ideas, JC: 32, 90, 94, 137, 154; KL: 49, 154, 184;
    P: 26, 104, 105; TP: 82, 90, 91; TT: 173, 176
and power, CH: 69; MJ: 76
and thought, TP: 73, 74
as seed, ASP: 59, 134-141; CH: 137; TP: 40 (see seed)
as Spirit's outlet in man, TP: 73, 74, 172, 173
as word, (see Christ, as word)
cannot express what God is, JC: 23
cells and, (see cells, and words)
consciousness and, TM: 63, 125; TT: 143, 144
constructive, MJ: 76
creative, MG: 13, 14, 17, 43, 44; MJ: 45; TP: 73, 74,
    80, 81, 173 (see creation; God, Word of)
    importance of faith in, JC: 15, 89, 144, 161, 163,
        175, 176; P: 47; TM: 29
each must use, for himself, JC: 98, 119; TP: 73, 74
entering fourth dimension (or kingdom of heaven)
    through use of, KL: 170, 171; TT: 127, 130, 131
every condition springs from the, CH: 137
every, is preserved in ethers, CH: 68, 69
formative vs. creative, TM: 29
fulfillment of may be delayed, JC: 47, 85
germ, JC: 88
God creates by power of His, KL: 166; TP: 77 (see
    God, as creator)
healing by use of, ASP: 71, 72; JC: 87, 89, 90, 91, 99,
    107, 144, 155; KL: 174; TP: 164-174; TT: 49, 143,
    150 (see healing, through power of word)
holding in mind, JC: 94
idle, CH: 64
"if a man keep my," ASP: 24, 30
intonation of, JC: 164
Jehovah as, (see Jehovah, as word)
Jesus and the, JC: 89-99, 132, 133, 144, 161, 162, 163;
    KL: 164, 166; MJ: 25, 135; P: 105, 112, 113;
    TM: 7, 62, 63; TP: 73; TT: 139, 171-178
Jesus Christ and the, JC: 88, 90, 91, 98, 109; KL: 20;
    TP: 28; TT: 173, 177, 178
man forms his world by power of his, KL: 154, 155;
    P: 80, 81; TP: 73-82
man justified or condemned by own, JC: 5, 15, 161,

174; KL: 75; MJ: 157

of God, MJ: 11, 65, 92, 93, 180; TP: 73, 77, 173
   as idea, ASP: 136
   as seed, ASP: 134-141

of praise and thanksgiving, JC: 137; P: 105; TP: 91

of Spirit, JC: 154

of the Lord, TM: 125

of Truth, ASP: 40; JC: 87, 88; KL: 196; MJ: 139;
   P: 184; TP: 20, 80

power of God available to man through his, KL: 73;
   TP: 77-82

power of spoken, ASP: 10, 24, 30, 37, 50, 54, 55, 84,
   128, 139, 141, 148, 149; CH: 63-70, 117, 136, 137,
   138; JC: 9, 14, 15, 16, 17, 47, 87-98, 119, 121, 123,
   132, 133, 137, 144, 154, 155, 161, 162, 164, 174;
   KL: 12, 17, 34, 71, 73, 74, 75, 76, 143, 153, 154;
   MG: 94, 122, 270, 364, 365; MJ: 54, 55, 76, 93,
   103, 104, 132, 135, 157; P: 13, 36, 37, 47, 48, 53,
   54, 103, 104, 105, 112, 148, 176, 184; TM: 18, 19,
   29, 30, 61, 62, 125, 166; TP: 4, 19, 21, 23, 27, 34,
   35, 40, 41, 71, 72, 73, 77, 80, 81, 82, 86, 90-92, 137,
   164-174; TT: 49, 52, 143, 144, 148, 149, 166, 171,
   172

prospering, P: 103, 104, 105, 112, 113; TP: 82

responsibility for, JC: 174

sacred, JC: 89, 90, 91, 92

salvation through, JC: 162, 175, 176

Scripture texts concerning, CH: 70, 71

soul molded by thought and, TP: 90

spiritual, JC: 89, 92
   body formed through use of, KL: 95, 166, 167;
      TT: 148, 149, 150

sure in action, JC: 112

"the lost," TP: 165

to keep, JC: 89, 90, 91, 93, 95

Truth affirmations for quickening and healing through,
   KL: 162, 167

two activities of the, ASP: 148

use or misuse of, JC: 89-92; TP: 40, 78, 79, 83, 86;
   TT: 150

written, JC: 88

words, CH: 65, 78, 79; JC: 90, 137, 174; KL: 166;
    TP: 34

work, JC: 112, 118; KL: 39, 106, 107; P: 32, 33, 111,
    114, 151, 155; TM: 112, 113, 123
  and redemption of man, JC: 98, 99
  faith in, P: 50
  foundation of every, P: 50
  God has sent each to do a certain, ASP: 96, 114, 115
  imagination and, P: 76, 77, 100, 101
  in sympathy with life principle, P: 139, 140
  in unity with God, JC: 143; P: 184, 185; TM: 27
  Jesus and, ASP: 18; CH: 98; KL: 51; MJ: 52, 53, 59,
    60, 135; P: 86
  of Holy Spirit in man, ASP: 99
  of man, (see *man, work of*)
  prosperity the result of, JC: 37, 39; P: 33, 34, 68
  praise improves our, CH: 79

works, KL: 15
  doing the greater, ASP: 11, 41
  good, P: 79, 150, 151
  Jesus and, ASP: 10, 11, 18, 19, 67, 71; MJ: 65, 105,
    111
  of God, ASP: 18, 19, 67, 68; MJ: 97, 105, 140;
    TM: 112, 113
  of Spirit, MJ: 57, 58, 111
  spiritual, JC: 167
    See also Jesus

world, ASP: 67, 68; JC: 121; MJ: 135, 150
  as created by God, TP: 73
    and the new dispensation, JC: 20
  "end" of, ASP: 162; JC: 20, 35, 149; KL: 26, 27, 40,
    41
  equal distribution of supply in, demonstrated by Jesus,
    P: 126-128
  evolution of, ASP: 85, 86; TM: 34, 120
  four-dimensional, P: 70, 71
  natural, and science, ASP: 60
  not ours to reform, TT: 127

of sense, ASP: 21
outer, CH: 100, 101; TT: 8
people of, leaving out God in zeal for solution of economic problems, TP: 128
to overcome, TM: 69
visible—invisible, KL: 102
welfare of, depends on its inhabitants, ASP: 52, 53
why does not God reform, ASP: 63
withdrawal from, MJ: 150
World War II, ASP: 29

worry,
and prayer, JC: 81
banishing, P: 110, 122
freedom from, JC: 142; P: 110, 122, 142; TM: 128
Jesus on, TM: 160
Truth statements for healing of, TP: 179
vs. confidence, ASP: 71

worship, JC: 74, 104; KL: 77, 123, 159, 160; MJ: 29, 30, 46, 48, 50, 99; TP: 139

wrestling, MG: 258, 369

writings, (see *Scriptures, writers of*)
sacred, JC: 87, 88, 122, 139, 140; TM: 116
secular, JC: 88, 122

wrongs,
forgiving, P: 117
righting, JC: 134

Y

Yahveh, meaning of name, TP: 165, 166

Yahweh, JC: 155; MG: 32, 33
  meaning of, JC: 141, 182, 183

Yeve, Hebrew word, KL: 111

young, MG: 138

youth, ASP: 101; KL: 13, 70, 162, 163; MG: 69, 70;
    MJ: 110; TP: 128
  affirmations for renewal of, KL: 13, 163
  eternal, MJ: 110

youthfulness, CH: 105

Z

Zaavan, MG: 287

Zacharias and Elisabeth, P: 44

Zaphenath-paneah; also, (Joseph), MG: 321

Zeal, TM: 130-141 (see *enthusiasm*)
   affirmation for regulating, KL: 160
   and genius, TM: 138, 139
   and religion, MJ: 29, 30, 153, 154
   as affirmative impulse of existence, TM: 130-132
   defined, ASP: 26; KL: 159
   direct but do not repress, TM: 132
   excessive, MJ: 29, 30
   Jesus on, TP: 128
   judgment and, TP: 126, 127
   Paul as a zealot, ASP: 27
   prosperity through, ASP: 35
   represented by Issachar, MG: 241, 275, 346
   represented by Simon the Canaanite, (Zealot), MG: 241;
      TM: 16, 22, 130-141; TP: 127, 128
   should be tempered with wisdom, ASP: 27; JC: 174,
      175; KL: 155, 159, 160; MJ: 29, 30; TM: 132, 133,
      140, 141, 153; TP: 127, 128
   spurs to action, ASP: 26, 27, 35; JC: 174; KL: 159,
      160; TM: 130, 131; TP: 126
   supply and, CH: 78, 79
   tempered with wisdom, ASP: 27; TM: 132-133
   use and misuse of, TP: 126-128

Zeboiim, MG: 102, 130, 131, 132 (city of the Plain)

Zebulun, (order), MG: 241, 242, 275, 346, 367

Zemarite, MG: 101

Zepho, MG: 279

Zerah, MG: 281 (son of Reuel), MG: 307, 345 (son of Judah)

Zibeon, MG: 277, 283, 284, 286

Zillah, MG: 63

Zilpah, MG: 235, 239, 275, 294

Zimran, MG: 201, 202

Zion, TP: 134

Ziphion, MG: 346

Zoar, or Bela, city of the Plain, MG: 126, 131, 167

Zohar
  father of Ephron, MG: 191
  son of Simeon, MG: 344

zone, spiritual, JC: 83, 84, 87

Zuzim, (people), MG: 132